Sara,
I'm grateful for your leadership and advocacy for people with disabilities and those who serve them. You are a champion.

Best wishes,
Thane

champion

"YOU'VE GOT THIS!"

Components of Person-Centered Planning

1. Valued and used by the person
2. In the person's possession
3. Clear, meaningful, achievable
4. Separate from record
5. Revised and updated regularly

The CQL Personal Outcome Measures

My Human Security

My Community

My Relationships

My Choices

A NEW PLAN

A NEW PLAN

Using Positive Psychology to
**Renew the Promise
of Person-Centered Planning**
for People with
Intellectual and Developmental
Disabilities

Art Dykstra
Thane Dykstra, Ph.D.

High Tide Press

Published by High Tide Press
101 Hempstead Place, Suite 1A
Joliet, IL 60433
HighTidePress.org
ANewPlan.org

A new plan:
Using positive psychology to renew the promise
of person-centered planning for people with intellectual
and developmental disabilities /
Art Dykstra and Thane Dykstra, Ph.D.

ISBN 978-1-892696-63-2

Printed in the United States of America

All proceeds from book sales
benefit the persons receiving supports
from Trinity Services, Inc.

Our heartfelt thanks to

Kim and Anita

for who and how they are.

Dedication

This book is dedicated to those individuals throughout the country
who have devoted their careers to helping others,
especially those who are working within the provider community.

We would like to thank the Board of Directors of Trinity Services:
Raymond McShane (Chairperson), Jan Agazzi, Chris Falvey,
Greg Geuther, Barbara Hall, Bob Libman, Barbara McGoldrick,
Ron Stricklin and Ken Stromsland; and also the members
of the Trinity Foundation Board: Charley Smith (Chairperson),
Robert Borgstrom, Klint DeGues, Mike Sieling, John Slack, Bob Taylor
and George Troha for their encouragement and support.
These individuals have been faithful supporters of Trinity and
are truly committed to helping others live their best life possible.

And finally, to those who have blessed our lives
and given us the opportunity to know and serve them.

Thank you,
Art and Thane

Table of Contents

Sign up for The PCP newsletter and many more resources
for Person-Centered Planning at ANewPlan.org

Preface

This book introduces a contemporary model of person-centered planning, "My Plan to Flourish," for individuals with intellectual or developmental disabilities. As will be seen, it is also applicable to planning for other people, such as the elderly and persons recovering from mental illness, who may also need supports in goal setting and task accomplishment.

The model is based on the research findings of positive psychology, best and promising practices, and the benefits that result from cultivating a positive, high performing work culture. It also recognizes the pioneering work done by John O'Brien, Connie O'Brien, Beth Mount, Michael Smull, and others in person-centered planning, especially with respect to significant issues, such as choice, autonomy, community membership, personal gifts and personal futures planning.

The book is primarily written for those staff members, whether case managers, qualified intellectual disabilities professionals (QIDPs), psychologists, social workers, behavior analysts, direct support staff, or managers and administrators, who are working to support people through provider organizations. We want to recognize their commitment, provide encouragement as they continue supporting others and acknowledge the great impact of their efforts. Thousands and thousands of people with disabilities are living a better life today because of their presence and outstanding efforts in organizations.

Other readers are also welcomed—parents, guardians, elected and appointed officials, academics, consultants, and others. We trust they too will work together with us to help bring about the systems changes that can further benefit those we seek to support. This book, however, is primarily intended for the staff, and especially champions, who are working every day to make a difference in someone's life.

CHAPTER 1

The Foundation:
A Person-Centered Culture

> "Would a bird build its nest
>   if it did not have its instinct for
>   confidence in the world?"
> —Gaston Bachelard

A Clarifying Perspective

The authors of this book are possibilists.[1] In other words, while we recognize the world that we live in includes many disheartening, discouraging dimensions, we believe in possibilities, that one can always do the next best thing and that progress is possible. As a friend and colleague, Dr. Timothy Williams has observed, "Nothing stops us from doing the next, simple, single doable thing." With that in mind, we are also optimists and place our bet on psychologist Carol Dweck's insight that **what people believe will shape what people achieve.**[2]

Hans Rosling, a physician, researcher and world-renowned public educator, shared an important observation that has influenced our thinking, when he noted that "things can be both bad and better" at the same time. In his book *Factfulness,* written shortly before his death in 2017, he offers the insights that follow.

However, before reading Rosling's observations, think about the field of disabilities and how we are bombarded every day with negative

> I am saying that **things can be both bad and better.**

messages—"People are still living in group homes," "People still don't have jobs," "People are still in sheltered workshops," "People aren't doing person-centered planning correctly," "People still don't have individual budgets," and the list goes on.

How to Control the Negativity Instinct

How can we help our brains to realize that things are getting better when everything is screaming at us that things are getting worse?

The solution is not to balance out all the negative news with more positive news. That would just risk creating a self-deceiving, comforting, misleading bias in the other direction. It would be as helpful as balancing too much sugar with too much salt. It would make things more exciting, but maybe even less healthy.

A solution that works is to persuade yourself to keep two thoughts in your head at the same time.

It seems that when we hear someone say things are getting better, we think they are also saying 'don't worry, relax' or even 'look away.' But when I say things are getting better, I am not saying those things at all. I am certainly not advocating looking away from the terrible problems in the world. **I am saying that things can be both bad and better.**

Think of the world as a premature baby in an incubator. The baby's health status is extremely bad and her breathing, heart rate, and other important signs are tracked constantly so that changes for better or worse can quickly be seen. After a week, she is getting a lot better. On all the main measures, she is improving, but she still has to stay in the incubator because her health is still critical. Does it make sense to say that the infant's situation is improving? Yes. Absolutely. Does it make sense to say it is bad? Yes, absolutely. Does saying 'things are improving' imply that everything is fine, and we should all relax and

not worry? No, not at all. Is it helpful to have to choose between
bad and improving? Definitely not. It's both. It's both bad and better.
Better, and bad, at the same time.

That is how we must think about the current state of the world.[3]

The "Bad" We Face

How can we apply Rosling's observations to the field of disabilities?
Since it is possible to entertain two thoughts in our heads at the
same time, we can acknowledge that some things are indeed bad,
while some others are better. Both can occur at the same time.
Let's consider some of what we categorize as bad.

Staffing Shortages

There is no doubt that the national shortage of direct support staff
available to work with people with disabilities is a major crisis, and
the prospects of improvement don't look terrific, even with state and
federal minimum wage increases. Community providers cannot
afford to be minimum wage providers. In fact, as we write this book,
companies are launching major recruitment efforts aimed at the entry
level employee, such as McDonald's "Archways to Opportunity."
Besides significant salary increases, the candidate can take free English
as a Second Language classes, earn a high school diploma, receive
college tuition assistance, take McDonald's courses for credit, participate in a no cost/low cost college tuition program at select
colleges, and receive free educational advising.[4] For providers to recruit
committed and talented employees, wages must be competitive and
indexed to a cost-of-living adjustment.

It should also be noted that the job requirements for direct support staff are much more demanding than those working as clerks in retail or as counter staff in the fast food industry. Today, our direct support staff are confronted with supporting people with major health issues and chronic conditions, and so they must be knowledgeable in nursing practices and medical care. In some instances, they are even administering medications.

Their duties are many—transportation, meal preparation, teaching self-help skills, assisting individuals in basic hygiene practices and carrying out individual support or behavioral plans. In addition, they are frequently called upon to work with people with very challenging behavior that can even lead to personal injury.

Furthermore, direct support staff must be skilled in interpersonal relations, including knowing when to respond, when to support and when to praise. Not only that, these staff must pass background checks, employment physical exams, complete required regulatory training, and pass the related tests, as well as be capable of documenting necessary clinical or program information as needed. This is not a job that can be done by anyone who just shows up.

Underfunding

Most readers recognize the reality that funding for human services is primarily dependent on Medicaid reimbursement. While state reimbursement rates vary, there is tremendous competition for those dollars along a wide array of needs. It is, indeed, rare for a governor to make human services funding—or for that matter, disability funding—a priority. But it's not rare for state-appropriated dollars to follow a crisis or newspaper exposé.

The field of disabilities has never been generously funded. While wage increases are of paramount importance, the reality is that operating costs continue to rise, whether they are associated with occupancy rates, insurance, utility costs or transportation. One can do more with less for only so long.

Insufficient funding clearly impacts the people being served or supported and can, indeed, be a significant barrier to goal achievement, whether it be employment, participation in recreation, affordable housing, or, for that matter, appropriate dental services. As suggested previously, inadequate funding clearly leads to inadequate staffing and increased staff turnover. Consequently, many more dollars are being spent on obligatory onboarding and preservice training activities rather than on in-service educational experiences.

Today, many providers are postponing needed building and equipment repairs; delaying vehicle replacement; cutting staff positions or freezing the filling of staff vacancies; and in some cases, decreasing services or closing programs.

Ruined by Regulation

No one—well, maybe a few people—faults regulatory bodies, whether the state or national bureaucrats, for wanting to keep bad things from happening. But, while regulations may address one "bad thing," they often end up making other things worse. Said another way, they usually see the trees but not always the forest.

This is not a job that can be done **by anyone who just shows up.**

A very specific example, discussed later in these pages, is the ever-increasing requirement to add more and more elements to the personal record, which usually has the individual's personal goals embedded in it somewhere. Many of the added items are important but do not have to be in a person's plan for the future. None of us, those writing this book or those reading it, plan this way, and then, of course, the question is asked, "Why aren't plans implemented?"

Person-Centered Record

- Assessments
- Health, Medical
- Legal
- Safety and Behavior Concerns
- History: Services and Supports
- Additional Supporting Materials

The current misapplication of the principle of being conflict free with respect to case management is still another example of good intentions gone wrong in terms of person-centered planning. For instance, rather than dealing with specific providers who might be operating with fixed service options, policy is implemented that prevents very capable providers from developing person-centered plans. In fact, they become implementers and now there is a coordination problem in the system. Regulators very frequently overwrite the regulations. As a result, "the entire class has to stay after school rather than the problem student."

Most individuals and families select providers based on their reputations in the community and on the quality of their interactions with those they serve. A very significant number of providers are capable of working with people in helping them craft a plan for a more desirable future while at the same time supporting them in day or residential services.

It is clear that an ongoing tension continues to exist between personal freedom and regulation protection, whether it be health and safety issues, data collection or documentation requirements. As Martin Seligman has observed in *The Hope Circuit* (2018), "Not getting it wrong does not equal getting it right."[5]

Managed Care

Whether it is persons with disabilities themselves, family members, or other stakeholders in the disabilities system, there is an awareness that the current disabilities services and supports approach needs improvement. Clearly, current Medicaid funding levels are not sufficient to provide high quality person-centered services and supports, let alone fund the individuals not currently served, many of whom are on waiting lists.

Looking at specific states in which managed care has been implemented does not provide much encouragement for the application of this model for the long-term support of persons with intellectual and developmental disabilities. Providers are obviously feeling the increased pressures of cost containment, and in some states, insurance companies are actually leaving the enterprise.

The uncertainty has caused many to begin asking questions:

- **How will insurance companies make a profit from an underfunded system?**
- **How will people with disabilities and their families participate in the design of a new system?**
- **Who advocates for person-centered planning and the intended outcomes in a managed care approach?**

Sad to say, managed care gone wrong looms as the next bad thing that's unfolding, or is on the horizon in many states.

The "Good" We See

Much of the early years of the person-centered movement emphasized what wasn't working. Some of the issues identified included people didn't have choice, were put in programs by providers, didn't have opportunities to live and work in the community, were in very large congregate settings, and treated as second class citizens. And the conclusions drawn about the people served in provider organizations was that what they were experiencing wasn't real living—wasn't real choice, community, autonomy or happiness.

Fortunately, a lot of distance has been covered since the early years of person-centered planning. We have made significant progress in moving from services to supports, from prevocational programs to real jobs, from very large institutions to a wide range of residential supports and alternatives. Even so, we can say with certainty that there are still more fights to fight and more obstacles to overcome, though we can take comfort in knowing things will get better if we believe they will and continue to work in that direction.

Better Things Are Happening

Trinity Services, an organization that has supported people with intellectual and developmental disabilities for nearly 70 years, has certainly experienced the bad, the good and the better. Among those bad experiences have been stories, common across the country, that could be labeled "Not in my back yard." Indeed, Trinity staff have even attended community meetings where both program participants and staff were physically threatened if a group home were to be located in that specific neighborhood. On the other hand, we can look around and find encouraging instances of positive shifts in attitude and behavior. Trinity provides a few specific examples of the better.

Trinity Services
New Lenox, Illinois

The organization is currently located in New Lenox, IL, a southwest suburb of Chicago with nearly 30,000 residents. The New Lenox mayor and elected trustees have been most supportive of Trinity for over 25 years. In 2012, Trinity was seeking a new home office building that could accommodate about 150 staff members. As it turned out, a building under construction in the town's Commons area became available. The Mayor of New Lenox, Tim Baldermann, invited Trinity to the Commons and remarked, "What better organization to be in the center of town than an organization that serves people with disabilities? It's where they belong." And so today, Trinity, along with the city municipal building, a very active public library, public safety building, and large, successful bank, is one of the main tenants of the city square. The people we serve, their families and our staff are all thriving in this environment.

The New Lenox Commons is a welcoming space with a circle walkway, pond and park environment. The city hosts annual events on the grounds, such as summer concerts and Christmas on the Commons, all of which actively include people with disabilities. It also serves as the starting point for Trinity's annual 5K fundraising event.

Mayor Baldermann, a compassionate leader, mentioned in the story above, is also a talented individual, in terms of political expertise and interpersonal relationships. He certainly has a heart for people. On the occasion we describe, Baldermann had recently won the mayoral election, and the Executive Director of Trinity had not yet had a chance to meet him. It was summertime, and the city was hosting its annual "Proud American Days" in one of the nearby park district areas. As the executive director was visiting the event, he came upon one of the people that Trinity was serving. The young man promptly asked the director, "Hey, do you want to meet the mayor?"

"Sure," responded the director, although he was somewhat doubtful about the outcome. The two walked together for a few hundred yards and came upon a man talking with a small group of people.

The young man stood politely near the mayor. Soon the mayor recognized him and addressing him by his first name said, "Hi, John. How are you doing?" It turned out the mayor had met him at a New Lenox store where he worked. And sure enough, John introduced the executive director to the mayor.

Mayor Baldermann has truly made a difference in the lives of many people with disabilities and their families, and some of the people served by Trinity are even his Facebook friends. His openness to them is just one example of those who are influencing their communities to reach out and invite people with disabilities to be fellow citizens and community members.

As is true in other organizations throughout the United States today, Trinity has been able to provide the people it serves with more job opportunities through its employment services than ever before. In addition, more people are moving to apartments and small settings.

On another positive front, more people are increasing their independence through assistive technology solutions that are discovered and implemented at Trinity's TEC Lab (Technology Enhancing Capabilities Lab). The TEC Lab was established to assist people with a variety of disabilities through identifying and implementing assistive technology solutions. TEC specialists help a person find a commercially available product or create solutions for independence in any aspect of their daily lives. These solutions can help increase or maintain their communication skills, mobility, safety or personal care, while maximizing their personal freedom.

In addition, it is most gratifying to attend such national gatherings as the National Association of QIDPs (NAQ) Conference or the Council on Quality and Leadership (CQL) Conference, and listen to and share in the positive life stories occurring across the country.

Clearly, things can be bad and better at the same time.

A Positive Culture: Getting Better Together

The authors strongly believe that organizations serving people with disabilities should want and need to create positive, high-performing, person-centered cultures that promote and strengthen efforts to support the people they serve in crafting a person-centered plan. This type of culture serves as the very foundation for developing the "My Plan to Flourish" introduced here.

One of the authors has discussed this important concept in *Creating a Positive Organizational Culture* (High Tide Press, 2016). The book focuses on how people work together to get things done, which is predicated on how we answer the question, "How do we want to be together?" Shared values are of utmost importance and guide the direction of the organization. At Trinity, values are tied to the mission statement, "Helping people live full and abundant lives."

Leaders at all levels of the organization operate within the framework of servant leadership, typified by behaviors based on the principle that "when we give, we receive." Collaboration is also at work and essential to team cohesiveness. Staff are working together because they want to and have a common, overarching purpose.

In a positive culture, care is given to hiring the best applicants because the fundamental reality is that our staff are the organization. Therefore, in a person-centered culture, employee relationships receive a great deal of attention. This is true both at the level of appreciation— the daily practice of gratitude—and courtesy, based on respect for who the other person is, and recognition—being cognizant of and expressing gratefulness for what a person does or accomplishes.

Furthermore, learning and personal growth are essential if the organization is to get better and go forward. As some have said, "If you're not growing, you're not going." Staff at all levels of the organization have opportunities for growth from targeted readings, classes, required and elective training opportunities, tuition reimbursement at local colleges and universities, as well as periodic on-site, graduate degree education programs.

Finally, there is an emphasis on optimism and having a positive outlook. Being with people who focus on the positive clearly increases personal positivity. Just as we seek to see the people we serve flourish, we also seek to see our employees flourish so that they too might live their best possible lives.

"If you're not **growing,** you're not **going**."

CHAPTER **2**

The Importance of Planning

"Planning is bringing
the future into the present
so that you can do
something about it now."
—Alan Lakein

Most people reading this book have participated in a variety of planning events—some because you wanted to, some because you had to. Older readers might find it interesting to wonder what the career record is for placing "Post-it" notes on walls or the white boards at planning meetings.

Depending on need, experience and the size of the board of directors and its members' interest, many organizations develop strategic plans that include a called-for timeframe with subsequent rollover dates, and other details. In some instances, the plans are followed, and in others they are put on a shelf and perhaps taken off to be referenced in the pages of a funding or foundation request. Those who wish to build truly successful operations must understand that strategic thinking is actually more crucial than the strategic plans themselves.

In a similar fashion, the same might be said for person-centered planning. Some plans are enthusiastically written, authentically crafted and fully implemented. Others are not. They are destined to live in a locked cabinet only brought to light for a purge. What is clearly vital is that we are working and thinking in a person-centered way.

What is clearly vital is that we are working and thinking in a person-centered way.

We are all familiar with planning efforts in our lives—people plan weddings, baby showers, vacations, the remodeling of a home and what they are going to do in their retirement. And there is no shortage of commercially available "planners," including the still popular paper planners that often come with expensive and impressive leather covers. In addition, technology has brought a surge in mobile smartphone apps. Some people use two or three planners at the same time. However, writing down or typing in the tasks that you want to accomplish doesn't make them happen.

What's intriguing in all of these planning efforts is how *infrequently* we seek to address or plan for the significant things in our lives.

Where are we going?

Why?

Are we living a life in
which we are flourishing?

How are our
significant relationships?

Should we make plans
to improve our marriage?

Should we make plans to find another
job or improve our happiness?

Reasons Why People Avoid Planning

It's rather amazing that so few people plan for the most important
things in their lives, and when someone says they do, the plans
are rarely written down. "It's in my head," they frequently respond.
In fact, according to most statistics, the average adult does not
engage in meaningful planning activities—and those who do make
plans and write them down number less than 2%.[6]

In our informal polls, the significant planning that does occur is generally around financial matters—saving money for a down payment on a car or home is the most frequent response. But, even in these circumstances, the parties do not often follow a budget. And, if New Year's resolutions are examples of good planning, we all know that doesn't work out so well either.

Understanding some of the reasons people do not engage in planning may be helpful. Some common explanations include:

I don't need a plan.

These individuals feel life is going all right, so elaborate planning is a waste of time. They are comfortable "winging it," and besides, no one knows what's going to happen in the future anyway.

I'm too busy.

These people seem to be overwhelmed much of the time. They might say: "I have things to do, a family to raise," "I just don't have the time to sit down and plan right now," "Once I get ahead on my bills, I'll put a plan together," or sadly, what is also reported, "With everything else going on in my life, I just don't want to think about it."

Not a good time.

Reasons given in this category include: "It's too late," "I just graduated from college and I need to pay off my student loans," "I wouldn't even know where to start," "I'm ___ (age) and it won't do me any good now," or "My plan is to keep on buying lottery tickets."

Author and speaker Kamran Akbarzadeh further summarizes the reasons we avoid planning as follows:

1. We are reactive rather than proactive.
2. We are not organized.
3. We are not self-disciplined.
4. We procrastinate.
5. We don't know how to plan effectively.
6. We think planning is a waste of time!
7. We are not patient.[7]

Adults with intellectual disabilities are no different from those without disabilities. Planning does not occur to them naturally, either.

The Planning Advantage

We share the following information so that those of you in a leadership or champion role (see Chapter 7) will be better prepared not only to assist the person for whom a plan is being crafted, but also those staff and friends around the person who may need some inspiration and convincing.

Dwight Eisenhower made the observation that "Plans are nothing, planning is everything." One way to start the conversation with a planning skeptic is to ask the question, "Are you where you want to be right now?" Assuming the person responds openly, he will generally indicate a serious goal or desire for the future—perhaps a better paying job, a financial objective, a relationship priority or education aspiration. Planning will further help in achieving any of these goals, but reaching any one of them is not likely to occur if life simply "happens" to you or to me.

"Plans are nothing, planning is everything."
—Dwight Eisenhower

There are also other arguments in support of planning.

Planning:

- Allows us to use our time more wisely.
- Helps us avoid being trapped in the present when we simply respond to emergencies and daily demands. Time in planning allows us to free ourselves from feelings of being overwhelmed in the moment.
- Enables us to put the future into perspective.
- Allows us to see more opportunities and possibilities in our lives.
- Allows us to have more control over our lives, to make better decisions and to be more self-determining.
- Increases our productivity.
- Causes us to ask the question, "What do we want to achieve, accomplish and focus on?"

Finally, we can ask the question, "What happens to me when I don't have a plan? Am I just getting by on luck?" Two popular but worth-repeating axioms apply in this context:

- "If you fail to plan, you plan to fail."
- "What doesn't get scheduled, doesn't get done."

Clearly, we need to set direction in our lives.

Planning with Persons Who Have Disabilities

Planning is the vehicle for working with people so they can live their best possible life. While a plan is the product of the support efforts, it's not the prize. The evidentiary test of the process is a higher quality life as testified to by the person who receives the supports. As such, the plan is never done, circumstances change and so do people. We all have experienced something that we thought we truly wanted, but we were disappointed when we got it. The essential focus of the planning process is to understand and clarify what the person needs and wants in his life. These findings will be translated into goals to which he has made a commitment of time and effort.

We recognize that "people with intellectual and developmental disabilities" is a rather broad description and includes people with different ability levels, gifts, life experiences, and levels of motivation with respect to the planning process. So planning will be accomplished much more quickly with some individuals than with others. In many situations, when people initially seek the assistance of a service provider, that provider is virtually a stranger to them, which can slow the process of adjustment, getting acquainted and designing appropriate plans. Some people are fortunate enough to have invested family and friends who can assist in accelerating the understanding of their dreams and desires. But others may begin services and have no one to assist them in articulating their dreams.

The method of planning proposed in this book relies on individually tailored meetings that use a common approach and format. It is unfortunate that, in some instances, staff members working to support a person do not "believe" in planning. Therefore, it behooves us to work with them, so they can come to appreciate planning in their lives and in those of others as well.

Here's a governing thought to keep in mind:

Did **good things** happen as a result of having a plan—that would not have happened without one?

CHAPTER **3**
The Origin of
Person-Centered Planning

"To understand the reasons,
you must first look at the origins."
—Anthony Hincks

There are thousands of staff working to support
persons with intellectual disabilities across the United
States and the world. Many of these individuals
have worked their entire careers in the context of a
"person-centered planning" environment within a
variety of settings—from schools and adult learning
programs to case coordination agencies and residential
alternatives. It's something they have always done.
This, of course, is not to suggest that "it" has always
been done correctly.

Like most social inventions, person-centered planning was not
suddenly discovered in a laboratory, college classroom or the pages
of well-crafted legislation. Rather, it emerged as a developmental
construct from the efforts of many individuals and groups, who were
working over a long period of time to improve the lives of people
with disabilities.

The beginnings of the person-centered movement can be seen in the 1960s when many individuals, parents, providers, academics and thought leaders began to question the effectiveness of the "medical model" in serving and supporting individuals with intellectual disabilities. Large, ever-growing institutions were the center of service delivery, where the emphasis seemed to be on efficiency and control. Heightened attention to the living conditions inside the institutions revealed overcrowding, medications being used for social control, rampant abuse and neglect, inadequate staffing ratios, and many other shortcomings. A video exposé in 1967, entitled *Titicut Follies,* brought greater media attention to the negative nature of institutional life, in this instance, a hospital for the criminally insane.

Titicut Follies

Later in 1972, a national audience viewed *Willowbrook: The Last Great Disgrace*, a television exposé filmed by ABC news reporter Geraldo Rivera. Willowbrook State School had come under greater scrutiny for its deteriorating conditions and dehumanizing practices exacerbated by its overcrowded conditions. In the late 1960s, it housed and "cared for" over 6,000 residents in living quarters designed for 4,000.

Willowbrook State School

While *Willowbrook* clearly had a major role in increasing public awareness of the mistreatment of people with intellectual disabilities living in institutions across the country, it was a parental lawsuit that influenced change on many levels. Changes included the ratcheting up of concerns regarding needed oversight with respect to institutional abuse and neglect, a greater appreciation for human rights, and the need and desire for smaller community residential options. The consent judgment of 1975 was used as a reference, if not a model, by many states seeking to improve the condition of their state institutions.

Discussions began to emerge with respect to all the dimensions of the service delivery system, including the use of diagnostic labels, the dominance of psychiatry in the "treating" of individuals with intellectual disabilities—then called mental retardation—and such matters as the need for specialized therapies, the need for vocational training and community presence. Residential care was now under the gun. In his 1964 publication, *Challenges in Mental Retardation*, Gunnar Dybwad makes the following observations:

> *The least amount of progress in the field of mental retardation during the past decade was made in the area of institutional care. Some of the reasons for this unquestionably lie in the fact that brick and mortar have a tendency of forcing upon a program a "strait jacket." Another inhibiting factor has been a strong anti-institutional sentiment expressed in low salaries, low allowances for maintenance, and low esteem for the institution as a helpful agency.*

> *With many progressive developments in community care, one can expect during the next decade increasing pressure for the upgrading and updating of residential facilities for the retarded. In the process, the following issues will have to be met: Shall we continue to build large institutions serving thousands of residents? What is the measuring stick for the "economical size" of an institution—ease of maintenance, flexibility in classification, easy availability of supporting medical services, or the specific treatment and training potential for the individual residents?*

> *Is it reasonable to set general limitations on the size of institutions for the retarded—less than 1,500, less than 500, less than 50—or must we begin to look at the problem of size in conjunction with specific functions, which in turn must be related to the needs of the residents? Is there an upper limit in size beyond which the therapeutic and training potential for the individual resident is distinctly decreasing?[8]*

This is also interesting in light of conversations today—almost 50 years later—regarding size and community.

In addition, one can see the emergence of person-centered planning in the thinking of Bengt Nirje, a scholar and activist. In a work entitled *Changing Patterns in Residential Services for the Mentally Retarded*, published by the President's Committee on Mental Retardation in 1969, Nirje introduces the concept of the "normalization" principle, a guiding principle passed into law in Sweden in 1967. The following observation, quoted from the above book, illustrates the thinking going all the way back to the 1960s.

> *My entire approach to the management of the retarded, and deviant persons generally, is based on the "normalization" principle. This principle refers to a cluster of ideas, methods, and experiences expressed in practical work for the mentally retarded in the Scandinavian countries, as well as in some other parts of the world.*
>
> *As expressed by N.E. Bank-Mikkelsen of Denmark, this principle is given in the formula **"to let the mentally retarded obtain an existence as close to the normal as possible."** Thus, as I see it, the normalization principle means making available to the mentally retarded patterns and conditions of everyday life which are as close as possible to the norms and patterns of the mainstream of society.*

Residential care was now **under the gun.**

This principle should be applied to all the retarded, regardless whether mildly or profoundly retarded, or whether living in the homes of their parents or in group homes with other retarded. The principle is useful in every society, with all age groups, and adaptable to social changes and individual developments. Consequently, it should serve as a guide for medical, educational, psychological, social and political work in this field, and decisions and actions made according to the principle should turn out more often right than wrong.[9]

Nirje goes on to identify some of the practical applications of the principle. It should be noted that what was being emphasized was not the normalization of the person, but rather the normalization of the environment.

Progress for persons with intellectual disabilities was occurring on two main fronts: in the public school system with related reforms and in the evolution of residential care. After years of deliberation and development, the federal government issued regulations in 1974 for Intermediate Care Facilities for the Mentally Retarded (ICF/MR). Noticeable in those regulations was the definition of **"active treatment"** that specified the following:

a. The individual's regular participation, in accordance with an individual plan of care, in professionally developed and supervised activities, experiences or therapies;

b. An individual written plan of care that sets forth measurable goals or objectives stated in terms of desirable behavior and that prescribes an integrated program of activities, experiences, or therapies necessary for the individual to reach those goals and objectives.

Another very influential thinker and scholar, Wolf Wolfensberger, was also working to improve and impact systems of support for individuals with intellectual disabilities. Accepting and further refining many of Nirje's observations, Wolfensberger and Glenn published "The Program Analysis of Service Systems, PASS," in the mid-1970s. This publication represented a systematic way of evaluating services from the perspective of the principle of normalization. Many states began to use the insights of PASS in developing program guidelines for the delivery of services.

The PASS checklist, "The Program Analysis of Service Systems," sought to evaluate the quality of service through the ranking of trained raters. Levels were generally rated from 1 to 5, but a few were rated from 1 to 6. Some of the PASS elements (next page) included:

The PASS Checklist

Physical Integration Mechanism
• Local proximity
• Regional proximity
• Access
• Physical resources
• Program-neighborhood harmony
• Congregation and assimilation potential

Socially Integrative Interpretations
• Program, facility and location name
• Function congruity image
• Building neighborhood harmony
• Deviancy image juxtaposition
• Deviancy program juxtaposition

Socially Integrative Program Structures
• Deviant staff juxtaposition
• Deviant client and other juxtaposition
• Socially integrative social activities

Age Appropriate Interpretations and Structures
• Facilities, environmental design and apt
• Personal appearance
• Activities, routines and rhythms
• Labels and forms of address
• Autonomy and rights
• Possessions
• Sex behavior

Culture Appropriate Interpretations and Structures
• Internal design and appointments
• Personal appearance
• Activities, routines and rhythms
• Labels and forms of address
• Rights

Developmental Growth Orientation
- Physical overprotection
- Social overprotection
- Intensity of relevant programming

Model Coherency
- Model coherency

Quality of Setting
- Physical comfort
- Environmental beauty
- Individualization
- Interactions

Ideology Related Administration
- Comprehensiveness
- Utilization of generic resources
- Consumer and public participation
- Education of the public
- Innovativeness

Human Science Orientation
- Ties to academia
- Research climate

Regional Priorities
- Deinstitutionalization
- Age group priorities

Manpower Considerations
- Staff development
- Manpower development

Internal Administration
- Administrative control and structure
- Planning process
- Program evaluation and renewal mechanism

Finance
- Financial documentation-extent
- Budget economy[10]

...by the mid-1980s, the concept of **person-centered planning began to spread across the country.**

Wolf Wolfensberger came to Illinois in the early 1980s and visited one of the three newly constructed state-operated, developmental centers that served persons with intellectual disabilities. At that time, these centers represented a significant improvement over such large institutions as the Lincoln and Dixon Developmental Centers. One of the new facilities consisted of 50 homes, all well-furnished with eight people living in each home, two to a bedroom. Wolfensberger decried the facility and characterized it as a "colony." Later he would berate state officials for wasting state resources on its construction.

Wolfensberger and Susan Thomas subsequently developed and published a similar evaluation methodology for human service organizations based on the tenets of social role valorization. They understood their work in social role valorization as a corrective system of thought and suggestions for addressing the plight of people devalued by society because of perceived, incurable or irreconcilable deviations from accepted normalcy.[11]

By the late 1970s and early 1980s, a number of separate but philosophically linked models of service planning emerged, including "Individual Design Sessions" (Jack Yates, Herb Lovet), "Personal Futures Planning" (Beth Mount), "MAPS Making Action Plans" (Marsha Forest), and "Twenty-Four Hour Planning" (Karen Green and Mary Kovaks). Each of these approaches reflected the unique thinking of the authors, but clearly emphasized the primacy of the persons receiving or seeking services and supports. **All of the contributors stress the importance of a person's strengths and gifts rather than their weaknesses.** Since that time, many other "person-centered" models have come on the scene. Perhaps the two foremost approaches were "Planning Alternative Tomorrows with Hope [PATH]" (Jack Pearpoint, John O'Brien, Marsha Forest) and "Essential Life Style Planning" (Michael Smull).

In 1987, John and Connie O'Brien published their *Framework for Accomplishment* that identified five quality of life dimensions:

- Sharing ordinary places
- Making choices
- Developing abilities
- Being treated with respect and having a valued social role
- Growing in relationships.[12]

Generally speaking, by the mid-1980s, the concept of person-centered planning began to spread across the country. Indeed, it was a movement designed to assist persons with disabilities so that they might enjoy a better quality of life and have greater control over their lives.

Enjoying life.

Person-centered planning is a philosophy and a way of life. Many elements of current thinking and best practices had their origins in the person-centered planning movement. Included are such ideas or activities as:

- Age appropriateness
- Individualized supports
- Community participation
- Wants as well as needs
- Choice
- Meaningful relationships
- Life satisfaction
- Inclusion
- Self-determination
- Social/personal inclusion
- Dignity of risk
- Things that matter
- Having a meaningful day
- Moving from services to supports
- Supported living
- People-first language
- Self-advocacy
- Active support vs. active treatment
- Circles of support
- Styles of learning
- Positive behavior supports
- Quality of life
- Social capital
- Personal outcomes
- Valued social roles

When we revisit the conditions in which people with intellectual and developmental disabilities were forced to live not too many decades ago, it is encouraging to realize that the men and women who worked tirelessly to improve their lot have made a difference. **Many in communities and government now understand that people with disabilities have desires, can make their own choices and contribute to those around them.** We simply need to provide them the opportunities the rest of us enjoy.

Readers seeking a current understanding of what's available in terms of resources to assist in person-centered planning are encouraged to check out the Inclusion Press catalogue online at www.inclusion.com.

Person-centered planning is a philosophy **and a way of life.**

CHAPTER 4
The Principles of Person-Centered Thinking and Planning

> "We miss big opportunities if
> we simply let the day happen to us."
> —Caroline Webb

As seen in Chapter 3, person-centered thinking began to emerge as a force against the limitations of the "medical model," but the leaders were also seeking to accomplish more than just the cessation of an inadequate approach. They were seeking to bring the wants and needs of people with disabilities to the forefront, so that they could help them live their best possible lives.

While person-centered thinking and planning may vary in format, style and emphasis, an analysis of the intent, background thought and planning objectives reveal some clear principles of this approach.

The Principles of Person-Centered Thinking and Planning

1. People want to experience their best possible life—to flourish.

2. People want to be in control of their lives—to experience autonomy.

3. Choice is an important expression of personal freedom.

4. Being in community is a vital aspect of a good life.

5. Contributing, producing, sharing one's life is essential to being fulfilled.

6. Exercising rights and responsibilities, being an active citizen brings a sense of belonging and acceptance.

7. Meaningful relationships and social connections are essential.

8. Planning with others starts with deep, genuine listening.

9. Plans that are written down and valued help people achieve their goals.

10. Person-directed plans are only as good as their implementation.

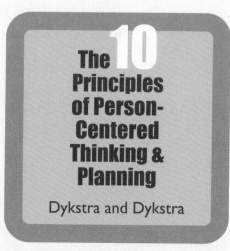

The 10 Principles of Person-Centered Thinking & Planning

Dykstra and Dykstra

The Principles Explained

1. People want to experience their best possible life—to flourish.
The goal of person-centered thinking and planning is to ensure that everyone, including people with disabilities, is living their best possible life. As unique human beings, it is apparent that the definition and standards of "best life" will vary from person to person. While living the best life is about the future, it also emphasizes the importance of today—right now—and allows us to **avoid being lost in yesterday or sidetracked by tomorrow.**

2. People want to be in control of their lives—to experience autonomy.
In the broadest sense, being in control of our own lives occurs when we can make decisions and choices that result in events and experiences happening in the way that we want them to. Control varies with circumstances. On a personal level, we feel more in control if we have a clear understanding of what we want. **Feelings of having control cause us to realize that we have a say in our lives,** and lead to greater self-satisfaction and more positive living.

3. Choice is an important expression of personal freedom.
Choice means that we can decide between at least two options or make a selection from two or more possibilities. Freedom of choice is a right that allows us to determine the course of our lives within the parameters of the law. **The ability to make our own choices not only provides independence, but it allows us to experience meaning in our lives.**

4. Being in community is a vital aspect of a good life.
The term "community" has many definitions. Most commonly, we use the term to describe a group of people living together in a particular place or site, a feeling of camaraderie or fellowship with others or individuals who have a common interest, such as a community of artists. Being in community means that one is experiencing meaningful relationships with a group of people that care about each other. Real communities provide a sense of belonging and trust. As John Swinton observed, **"To be included, you just need to be present. To belong, you need to be missed."**[13]

5. Contributing, producing, sharing our life is essential to being fulfilled.
Dignity, self-respect and a sense of fulfillment come to be when
a person is adding value to others, making a difference in their lives.
Furthermore, **being productive, achieving positive results and
being useful are sources of joy.** Research confirms that giving does,
in fact, make us happier than receiving, and it also allows us to feel
less vulnerable.

**6. Being an active citizen by exercising rights and responsibilities
brings a sense of belonging and acceptance.**
Being an active citizen means that you care about the community you
live in and are willing to work to make it better by helping on
projects, volunteering, voting or even serving on a committee. It's been
said that an active citizen is one who fulfills both his rights and
responsibilities in a balanced way. **Relationships are the essence of
community.** Doing things with others, doing things for others and
having others do things for us makes it work.

7. Meaningful relationships and social connections are essential.
As Martin Seligman has pointed out, **"Other people are the best
antidote to the downs of life and the single most reliable up."**[14]
Gratitude is also seen as a relationship-strengthening emotion that,
like optimism, influences our relationships, career and health.
Generally speaking, gratitude is expressed outward to others and
thankfulness is an inner expression of appreciation.

8. Planning with others starts with deep, genuine listening.
This message on a T-shirt offers us a little insight into listening well:
**"Not being able to speak is not the same as not having anything
to say."** Said simply, we should probably speak less and listen more,
especially when we are helping people make plans for their lives.
Not only is it important to be present in the moment, we must also
pay attention to body language and sense the feelings being expressed.
And we have to be careful that we ourselves aren't answering
the questions being asked of a person seeking assistance. Just because

someone is quiet while others are talking doesn't mean we can assume he has nothing to say. Goal achievement is dependent upon effective communication.

9. Plans that are written down and valued help people achieve their goals.

Research reveals that planning and writing down goals pay off in our lives. People with written plans fail less and accomplish more. As one observer has remarked, **"Imagine your written goals as a map or GPS system."** In other words, they provide us with a guidance system. It is best when goals are specific, have timeframes and, if possible, appropriate deadlines. Having a written plan that you can refer to is noteworthy in that it helps us take action. They can even include pictures, photography and videos. A plan serves as a reminder. It's also a way in which we can track our progress.

Finally, it is important that the plan that has been developed is valued by the person. His words and actions should also indicate that it reflects his values, and is important, beneficial and helpful.

10. Person-directed plans are only as good as their implementation.

Implementation means to carry out an intended action, to engage in the process of achievement. Person-centered plans are of no value if no action is taken to achieve goals and sustain them. **The worst thing that can happen when we are supporting someone is to develop a plan that has energized him for the future and then not carry it out.** In this instance, everyone is hurt who participated in the process.

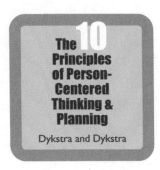

The 10 Principles of Person-Centered Thinking & Planning

Dykstra and Dykstra

CHAPTER 5

The Meaning of "Your Best Possible Life"

"Believe that life is worth
living and your belief
will help create the fact."
—William James

All of us want to live our best possible life—viewing the world and what we are experiencing in a positive fashion, enjoying today and looking forward to tomorrow. To be sure, there are individual differences. Some of us want to live in cities, others in the countryside; some want to be married, others to remain single. Some people want to experience all four seasons while others just want a tropical environment. We all have different priorities for what we want in life.

So what leads to the experience of a fulfilled life? Crossing off the things on our to-do list doesn't do it; worrying and fretting doesn't do it; trying to live someone else's life doesn't do it; and working on a bucket list doesn't do it. What does do it?

The ideas expressed in these pages introduce a new model of person-centered planning, predicated on the findings based on the research being done in positive psychology. In doing so, the idea or goal of living "your best possible life" is founded on the construct of well-being. Well-being is measured and defined by its elements, which contribute individually to our well-being in and of themselves.[15]

"Your best possible life" is founded on the construct of **well-being.**

Because the elements of well-being are so critical to the development of the person-centered planning approach introduced here, the following explanatory narrative closely follows the work of Martin Seligman in his book, *Flourish* (2011). The five elements he outlines are each chosen freely by people for their own sake. While they contribute to a person's well-being, they can be defined and measured independently. The five elements are **P**ositive emotion, **E**ngagement, **R**elationships (positive), **M**eaning and **A**ccomplishment/achievement (PERMA).[16]

Based on the work of other researchers, (not, however, included in the original model), a sixth element has been added to the umbrella construct of well-being— Health. The six elements are now referred to as PERMAH.

Positive Emotion
Engagement
Relationships
Meaning
Accomplishment
Health and Vitality

The Elements of Well-being from Positive Psychology

Positive Emotion

Everyone wants to feel good, but in positive psychology, this is different from merely having happy feelings. Generally speaking, it posits that emotions are feelings that we cannot create on our own. Another set of researchers hold that emotions are responses to a situation or a person. Whether they are one or the other, **positive emotions open us up, expand our awareness of the world, increase our options and help us enjoy life more fully.** Finally, research indicates that they correlate with greater physical health, increased longevity and a resistance to depression.

On the most popular list of positive emotions would be words, such as:

- Satisfaction
- Hope
- Cheerfulness
- Enjoyment
- Happiness
- Contentment.

Engagement

Most frequently, this element of well-being is defined in the context of **being immersed in a task or activity so intensely that time seems to have vanished.** Engagement occurs when we are totally absorbed or taken by our work, music, hobby or friendship. It is also very personal and experienced differently. For some, it could be their jobs and for others the enjoyable aspects of their lifestyle.

Seligman explains that engagement, as flow, results in a loss of self-consciousness in the moment, during an absorbing activity. It should be noted that this is reported after the absorbing event has concluded, not during the action.

Relationships (Positive)

Relationships and social connections are vital to our feelings of being alive. As Chris Petersen, a renowned researcher, has said, "Other people matter." Positive relationships occur when the two individuals in a relationship contribute to its success—good things go both ways. The coming together results in both partners feeling good about themselves and each other. Research also shows that focusing on the good in relationships, rather than the bad or negative, strengthens them over time. As might be expected, friendships come more readily to positive people and are also a source of happiness.

Meaning

Seligman defines this element as **"belonging to and serving something that you believe is bigger than the self."**[17] Once again, meaning is individually defined and experienced. Many of us find it in our work, relationships, volunteering or spiritual pursuits, such as helping others or serving God. We feel that our lives have a purpose. We are living for something outside of our own personal agenda. Meaning brings us fulfillment and a sense of significance because we are achieving what is valuable.

There are a couple of questions that quickly emanate from this element: "Are we realizing meaning in our lives? Are we experiencing meaning in our lives?" What we know from current research is that people who report having meaning are happier and healthier than those who don't. It should be noted that, in this context, we are referring to personal meaning, not how we answer the question, "What is the meaning of life?" (although watching the now classic Monty Python movie may prove beneficial to some readers).

Accomplishment/Achievement

The element of accomplishment/achievement rests on the notion that we are engaging in, working on or attempting something that has not been completed. It leads to a positive sense of fulfillment. **When we attain our goals, cross the finish line or hit the target, we experience a satisfaction that is exhilarating.** Some authors distinguish between achievement, a measurement against an external standard, and accomplishment, which refers to an internal, personal standard or goal.

Health

This element pertains to how a person describes his health, including **energy levels and vitality.** As you might expect, health is not just the absence of disease; it is also about being physically active and having a healthy lifestyle along with adequate rest. (*This is particularly important for persons with intellectual and developmental disabilities, who unfortunately are more likely to be living a sedentary lifestyle.*)

Putting It All Together: Flourishing

It can be said that we as people are flourishing in our lives if we are living and experiencing the six elements just discussed. However, flourishing is not a personal characteristic, such as height or weight, nor is it "present or not present" in our lives. Rather it is a process we engage in that promotes the good life through balance and goal setting.

The world of plants readily illustrates how we can identify the character of flourishing. Picture, for instance, a houseplant with shiny, lush leaves and fragrant blossoms. We can tell it is flourishing. On the other hand, picture a plant that is wilting or yellowing. It has leaves with spots or darkened areas and may even be stunted in its growth. We would quickly agree that it was languishing. How much better it is to be flourishing!

Let's think a little more about "living our best possible life." By starting with an understanding of well-being and the six elements of flourishing, we establish the platform for convergent development with respect to person-centered thinking and planning, especially as it relates to goal setting. The first steps in assisting individuals, who wish to experience greater flourishing in their lives through a person-centered plan, would be to have a series of conversations with them to ensure that they understood the six elements to the best of their ability.

> The first steps in assisting individuals would be to ensure that they understood the six elements **to the best of their ability.**

As might be expected, full understanding of the six elements of well-being will occur over time as the people receiving support become more familiar with the elements and their specific applications and relevance to their lives. For example, the experience and personal understanding of meaning may unfold over years. It is not just a simple answer to a question.

Dialogue regarding the importance of well-being in seeking to live a fulfilled life is obviously important. We recommend that provider organizations conduct classes for the people they support to further strengthen their understanding of well-being. Classes for staff are also critical, not only for their own personal benefit but also to better equip them to assist individuals actively seeking to carry out their "Plans to Flourish."

For those individuals who have good reading skills, the ability to grasp abstract concepts and a desire for feedback about their experience of flourishing, we suggest using the PERMA-Profiler devised by Butler and Kern (2016). It measures the pillars (elements) of well-being by identifying 23 questions to which a person responds using the numbers 1 through 10, 1 being "not at all" and 10 being "completely." It is likely that a staff person may be needed to assist the person in completing the questionnaire either by reading the questions or explaining some of the concepts.[18]

On completing the questionnaire, a staff member should dialogue with the person receiving assistance with the planning function to determine if there are any specific personal areas that he might wish to address and improve through the goal-setting process.

We also suggest that staff interested in furthering their knowledge of well-being complete the questionnaire as well. There is no charge and participants can take the assessment online and receive the scored assessment and report.

Other Important Considerations

The "My Plan to Flourish" model is clearly predicated on the research findings of well-being. Exploration and full attention to the six elements of well-being is critical to crafting a person-centered plan that will lead to the best possible life.

The CQL Personal Outcome Measures®

In addition, we strongly suggest that the "My Plan to Flourish" include an assessment of the person's desires and goals based on the Personal Outcome Measures® as developed by the Council on Quality and Leadership (CQL).[19] (See www.c-q-l.org/the-cql-difference/personal-outcome-measures.) These personal outcomes are valuable as they were garnered through national focus groups comprised of people with disabilities, who reported what was most important to them.

It is recommended that staff conducting CQL interviews follow the guidelines established by the CQL. The process culminates in determining the presence or absence of the outcome or enabling supports. This is most helpful in the planning process since it **enriches the dialogue with the person receiving supports with respect to identifying priority goals.** It is critical in the growth process that any outcomes recorded as "not present" be viewed as opportunities for future growth rather than personal failures.

The CQL Personal Outcome Measures

My Human Security
People...
1. Are safe
2. Are free from abuse and neglect
3. Have the best possible health
4. Experience continuity and security
5. Exercise rights
6. Are treated fairly
7. Are respected

My Community
People...
8. Use their environments
9. Live in integrated environments
10. Interact with other members of the community
11. Participate in the the life of the community

My Relationships
People...
12. Are connected to natural support networks
13. Have friends
14. Have intimate relationships
15. Decide when to share personal information
16. Perform different social roles

My Choices
People...
17. Choose where and with whom to live
18. Choose where they work
19. Choose services

My Goals
People...
20. Choose personal goals
21. Realize personal goals

The 21 Personal Outcomes clearly work synergistically with the elements of well-being, and when included in the person-centered planning process, increase the likelihood of a valued and meaningful plan.

In summary, three bodies of knowledge are being assembled and used to craft "My Plan to Flourish."

1. The principles of person-centered thinking and planning that highlight issues, such as choice, autonomy, a focus on strengths, relationships and community, among others.

2. The six elements of well-being: positive emotion, engagement, relationships (positive), meaning, accomplishment/achievement and health.

3. The 21 Personal Outcome Measures® as developed by the CQL.

We recommend that the people supporting a person with intellectual and developmental disabilities be quite familiar with these reference materials. This is especially important when working together to assist in the crafting of the necessary supports and the person-centered planning document. Champions or facilitators of the planning process, if available, or other support personnel for the person need to be competent and well-trained in these systems of thought.

CHAPTER **6**

The Essential Components
of a Person-Centered Plan

"If the wind will not
serve, take to the oars."
—Latin proverb

Today, everyone you talk to in the disabilities field
tells you that they are doing person-centered planning
and, in fact, have been doing it for years. They might
be. Some are and some aren't. There are all kinds of
models and formats to choose from: versions of
individual educational plans, newsprint and wall chart
options, plans that involve shapes and drawings,
video formats, and now mobile applications. In addition,
most states have created their particular and
favored "PCP" version that seems to have more of a
regulatory than a life-guiding value. One thing is
sure; with the prevalence of computerized forms,
tablets (e.g., iPad and Android), smartphones,
cloud storage (e.g., Dropbox and iCloud), and portable
printers, the plans have become longer and seemingly
all-encompassing.

As many people—including national experts, family members, providers and professionals— have observed across the country, **the problem is that well-intended, person-centered plans are not being carried out or implemented even when they are positively crafted.** (The implementation dilemma is discussed in Chapter 9.)

One thing is sure; with the prevalence of computerized forms, plans have become longer and **seemingly all-encompassing.**

The person-centered plan, identified in this book as "My Plan to Flourish," is the key document that serves as the written communication conduit for what a person desires for her life. It is for this reason that we are presenting the five essential components of a person-centered plan regardless of the format or approach. As will be discussed later, the failure to implement a plan can be easily traced to the lack of adherence to these essentials.

The Five Essential Components

1. The person-centered plan that is developed is valued, referred to and used by the person for whom it was developed.
2. The person-centered plan is in the person's possession.
3. The goals of the person-centered plan are clear, meaningful and achievable.
4. The person-centered plan is concise, readable and separate from a person-centered record.
5. The person-centered plan is revised and updated at regular intervals.

Components of Person-Centered Planning

1. Valued and used by the person

2. In the person's possession

3. Clear, meaningful, achievable

4. Separate from record

5. Revised and updated regularly

Discussion

1. The person-centered plan that is developed is valued, referred to and used by the person for whom it was developed.

Sadly, it seems that in many, many conversations with persons who have a person-centered plan of their own, we hear remarks, such as

I hate it.

I don't like it.

I find it useless.

It's demeaning.

It's a waste of time.

Sometimes they are upset with the process, the facilitators, the meeting conveners or the format of the plan itself. Not surprisingly, the most reflective individuals find the statement, "Here's a printout of your computer-generated plan," very offensive. In fact, many people receiving supports recognize that "their plan" looks just like everyone else's. The only difference is that their picture is on the cover.

So here's a question to consider:

How many times has a person with a disability—and with whom you have a support relationship—come up to you and asked to talk about her plan?

2. The person-centered plan is in the person's possession.
While most staff members who support individuals with disabilities would agree that people receiving services should have a copy of their plan, it's disturbing how many do not have any copy at all. And if they are aware that a copy exists, they may not know where it is kept. They might surmise that their parents have it, or that it is locked up in the med cabinet. Worse yet, it might have been thrown out. Clearly, people should have a copy of their plan, readily available for use.

3. The goals of the person-centered plan are clear, meaningful and achievable.
The core ingredients of the plan are each person's desired goals for the future. These objectives should be personal and reflect an appropriate span of time for accomplishment. In addition, staff members who support persons with disabilities should understand the intent. Goals—and the steps that have been outlined to achieve them—should be reviewed regularly.

Likewise, it should be noted that a person's plan for the future is not a personal care plan as originally conceptualized in the ICF/MR regulations along with the familiar standards of active treatment. There is a clear difference between caring for someone following the directives of professionals (which are necessary under some circumstances) and having a plan through which a person seeks to live their best life possible.

4. The person-centered plan is concise, readable and separate from a person-centered record.

One disadvantage of many of today's person-centered plans is their size and weight. People receiving services and supports are not interested in having a plan that resembles the three-inch thick yellow phone books of days gone by. Unfortunately, computers haven't made the product any better. It is now much easier to regurgitate assessment information, regulatory requirements, environmental expectations and—for the avant-garde—Ancestry.com or 23 and Me information. **Quite frankly, what matters the most to a person receiving supports can easily be lost in the midst of 20 or more pages.**

It is not unusual to find a person's goals for the future mired in a narrative reflecting the results of their annual review, which is frequently labeled an Individual Support Plan. Searching for genuine personal goals is like looking for a needle in a haystack, and there is plenty of hay: signature pages, contact information, assessments, rights statements, safety and protection from harm considerations, skill objectives, behavioral objectives if necessary, and if there is no family involved, perhaps a notation regarding pre-arranged funeral plans. Goals, when found, often follow the language formula, "Martin will increase his vocational skills—by a year from now" or "Martin will increase his independence in self-help skills—by a year from now." Will he actually do so? Does he want to?

Therefore, we take the strong position that person-centered plans should be a stand-alone document, separate from a person-centered record. The person-centered record is the document that should contain consents for release of information and other legal documents, and detailed medical information, along with any additional important items.

5. The person-centered plan is revised and updated at regular intervals.

Finally, plans should be in constant view if those receiving support so desire it—perhaps on the top of a chest of drawers. Persons supported should also be in ongoing discussions with their champions—whether parent, friend, facilitator or staff member—regarding their progress. In addition, it is important to recognize that a goal may be dropped, revised or adapted should plan holders initiate and direct such a change.

A Reminder

These Essential Elements are critical to the implementation and achievement of any goals identified.

CHAPTER **7**

Planning to Flourish

"If you don't know WHY,
you can't know HOW."
—Simon Sinek

In this chapter and the next, we address the
development of a contemporary approach
to person-centered planning: "My Plan to Flourish."
However, before beginning, it is important to
review three of the fundamental principles that
pertain to the planning function of the new model.

1. Plans must truly reflect the wants, needs and hopes of
   the persons for whom they have been developed, and are
   therefore valued by them. In other words, they like
   their plans and frequently talk about them with others.

2. The plans are in the possession of the persons receiving support. As will be shown below, they are constructed in such a manner that anyone—including the person for whom it is designed—can easily recognize it. Further, it is concise but sufficient to guide supports, and easy to update or modify as circumstances and events change. We must remember that all of us are continuously changing our minds and priorities, and most don't wait for our birthdays or annual "meetings" to update our journey.

3. The goals are clear, meaningful and achievable. Indeed, the goals and/or steps required to reach the desired end should be measurable but not cumbersome or staff-support intensive. It is important not to include or confuse a need for service improvements or responsibilities with the person's personal goals. For example, having more choice opportunities for meal selection or typical household activities is the responsibility of the service provider, not the person receiving supports.

The Discussion Context

For the discussion of the "My Plan to Flourish" model, we have chosen to use the example of a person who has a modest reading level, an intellectual disability and significant medical concerns. We present it in this context so that the description is less complicated by the many adaptations or modifications required to support, for instance, individuals without language, those without sight or hearing, or those with very significant physical impairments. Readers working to support persons with more significant disabilities are encouraged to study this model so that they understand the intent, the plan components and underlying rationale. This understanding will enable them to devise the appropriate adaptations.

The authors contend that even individuals without language or the ability to read should have in their possession a plan following the out-line of this approach. If family members are engaged, they should have a copy as well as those who will be helping to support the person in carrying out the goals.

While we recommend that every person have a "My Plan to Flourish" that follows the approach being described in this book, it is certainly acceptable for those who would benefit from or desire it to create a pictorial summary of the plan by having, for example, a photograph(s) or cutout pictures fastened to 8½" x 11" cardstock that a person recognizes and can point to.

An Important Acknowledgment

Hopefully, most readers are familiar with the work of people like Michael Smull, Beth Mount, John O'Brien and Connie O'Brien, and other pioneers in the person-centered movement. If not, you should educate yourself in their philosophy and suggested practices because their writings offer valuable orthodoxy. In fact, the counsel of John O'Brien with respect to issues, such as the importance of competent facilitation and the crucial role of "circles of support," represents the gold standard. Unfortunately, as noted earlier, the pursuit of the gold standard seems to be waning perhaps because of a lack of commitment, competing priorities, current funding levels, misguided regulations and now extreme staff shortages.

However, one thing cannot be ignored. While some of the alternative paths of person-centered accomplishment may vary and not be ideal, the "why" cannot. Beth Mount explains:

> Personal futures planning is an approach for learning about people with disabilities and creating a lifestyle that can help people contribute in community life. Personal futures planning is much more than a meeting; it is an ongoing process of social change. The effectiveness of a plan depends on a support group of concerned people who make a dream reality by learning to solve problems, build community and change organizations together over time. The locus of change is moved away from the person with a disability toward change in social roles, responses, and existing organizational structures.[20]

Providers can carry out person-centered planning with integrity within the resources they have with the help of support circles and dedicated employees, even as they work to find more funding as they go along. Sometimes these actions will reflect the "next best approach" rather than the ideal.

Unfolding Person-Centered Planning

In its origins, person-centered planning was created when caring and interested people came together on a voluntary basis and made a commitment to assist a person needing supports. Sometimes, the need was urgent.

In *Person-Centered Planning: Helping People with Disabilities Achieve Personal Outcomes*, Mary Mercer provides an excellent description and overview of the planning experience. It should be noted that, in revised editions, "the team" has been replaced by the volunteer circle of supporters. This is, no doubt, the most common experience today in the United States, especially in Medicaid-funded programs. Those interested in learning more about person-centered planning would benefit from reading Mercer's book.

Mercer introduces the planning process as follows:

> *Person-centered planning is not about taking standard service packages off the shelf.* **Rather than trying to fit people into existing service models and solutions, it allows a person's dreams and desires to guide the planning process.** *A dream is more than a goal or objective in a plan. It is what a person wants out of life! Dittmeier and Kleinert recommend service providers use four strategies when supporting people in identifying their vision of the future.*

> *First, they should describe the vision in great enough detail to give direction to the support team. For example, "getting more friends" is not specific enough to assist the team in developing supports. "Finding a girlfriend who likes to dance and go to funny movies," on the other hand, gives the team ideas about how to pursue the goal.*

> *Next comes describing a life that reflects the preferences and personality of the person—not a list of services. For example, supported employment is a service; working in an auto repair shop is a career choice.*

> *Another step is to think beyond what is currently obtainable and consider the question, "What does the person desire?" For example, a person currently lives in a group home with seven other people. She wishes to live in an apartment with one roommate (desired).*

Once the desired goal is identified, participants in the planning process must determine the steps to attain it.

Finally, the team must evaluate the planning effort by asking whether others would want to live the vision they have described.[21]

Imagine that the vision statement belongs **to you.**

Team members should imagine that the vision statement belongs to them. Does the vision describe a full life that they would want? Is the language appropriate for a person without a disability? If the language in the vision would only apply to a person who has a disability or a person who lives in a group home, then the vision is too narrow and is likely not person-centered. For example, if a person expresses a desire to have a job and earn money working at a grocery store, being placed in a janitorial crew, working at a sheltered workshop or attending a pre-vocational program doesn't meet the criteria of person-centeredness. Much thought must be given to the question of what the person would want to be doing if there were no current job openings at a local grocery store. The issue is clearly a team support activity.

Letting go of a disability mindset can be challenging for many teams. Too often, we plan in the context of the service system of which we are a part, fitting the person into a familiar context. Clues that we have planned with a system in mind include language, such as "community outings," "challenging behavior," "supervision," "activities," "family visits" or using the word *staff* in the vision statement. The vision should use everyday language, not jargon, and it should sound like a vision that you might identify for yourself.

Planning and Designing Supports

Using what everyone has learned about the person, the team can identify the priorities. They must compare how she wants to live with how she is currently living. Their next step is to determine:

- Things the person wants to learn to do to reach her dream
- Things others need to know or do in order for her to get what is important
- Things others need to know or do to help her stay healthy and safe.

A basic assumption of person-centered planning is that people are ready to do whatever they want with adequate supports. Helen Sanderson recommends that independence be measured, not by the number of tasks that people can do without assistance, but by the quality of life they can have with whatever support they need.[22]

It is possible to look beyond agencies, programs and formal sources of support. The service world may not be the best way to meet the person's every need. Rather than trying to fit people into existing service models, the team can determine what the person needs and then go about trying to locate or develop the support. Supports can include the following.

Personal Resources

These include a person's skills, competencies, characteristics and gifts. Most people have to build on personal strengths and capacities to reach their dreams. Often, teaching the person a new skill is the fastest, most appropriate support. Staff should use tested methods of structured learning experiences to build on her strengths and capacities. However, when learning demands will delay or prevent attaining her vision, other people, technology or services might better support her, at least for the present.

Independence
is measured,
not by the
number of tasks
that people
can do without
assistance,
but by the quality
of life they
can have with
whatever
support they
need.

Other People

Everyone needs support to reach their dreams; we differ only in the amount and kinds of support. Some of us are lucky enough to obtain support from a spouse, sibling, best friend or neighbor. Others depend on paid staff for part or all of their support needs. The team should look for ways to connect the person to her community and natural supports, those people who are not paid to help her (i.e., family, neighbors, fellow parishioners, coworkers, and so on).

> Everyone needs support to reach their dreams; **we differ only in the amount and kinds of support.**

Technology

Are there adaptations to the environment or task that will compensate for a person's disability? Determine if technology could enable her to perform work, daily living or leisure activities needed to reach her dreams.

Services

Determine if there are generic supports, such as a cab, city bus or carpool that can be used rather than specialized services (e.g., agency van driven by staff). Could a coworker teach the person the job rather than a job coach? The person-centered plan documents the support an individual requires to achieve her vision. However, support plans should be seen as evolving and flexible. Every person's future changes direction as life happens. Aspirations change and development occurs with new experiences, requiring adjustments in the pattern of supports and services. The team will need to reflect continually on successes and failures, try new things, resolve conflicts, and shift directions.

In all likelihood, the person-centered planning meetings will be chaired by a staff member from the provider organization. The staff member, who could be a case manager or qualified intellectual disabilities professional (QIDP), would hopefully serve as the champion for the person as the plan is carried out. The case manager or QIDP would also be responsible for putting the plan together as indicated in this narrative.

The Role of the Champion

As was just noted, the common practice today in the service environment is to mobilize a team around a person seeking or receiving services and supports. The purpose is to create a plan to help her enjoy a more desirable future while attending to her needs and wants. In ICF/DD environments, this is usually an interdisciplinary team, while in "waiver" settings, the teams go by a variety of names, from "waiver teams" to "support teams," and other similar designations.

The team to be led certainly includes the focus person and those she invites—family members, friends, and relevant staff members. In addition, **whenever you see a team, you should also see a champion.** The term "champion" is used to describe the primary person working to assist the person receiving supports, especially in helping her achieve the identified goals. This individual may also be responsible for scheduling the planning meeting, making sure minutes are taken, and all rules and regulations are followed. On occasion, the champion may not be a member of the team that developed the plan being implemented. Interestingly, certain business environments incorporate an actual position identified as "Implementation Specialist," an employee who works to execute plans and coordinate the achievement of successful outcomes.

The champion or meeting facilitator is typically a staff member with a number of persons on her "case load." This is a significant issue inasmuch as the larger the "case load," the more difficult it is to provide individual attention and supports. The situation becomes even more difficult when the person—whether a social worker, case manager or QIDP—also wears a supervisory hat for either a residential or day program setting. Those duties will complicate the champion role. Remember that in the circles of support approach, facilitators or chairpersons are not encumbered by other job duties or significant responsibilities. Rather, they are free to assist the people they support in carrying out their goals.

The chairperson identified above may, indeed, serve as the focus person's champion, but this is a role defined by the actions taken and results achieved. It is not just a job assignment or position held. For example, we all know that some team leaders are not leaders of teams—just as wearing a baseball hat doesn't make one a baseball player. However, champions, more than likely, choose this role because they are interested and engaged in matters of personal growth and learning not only for themselves but also for others.

It is important that organizations provide the necessary training so that champions are comfortable with, competent in and understand the three knowledge platforms: PERMAH, CQL Outcomes and the Person-Centered Principles. In addition, they should use deep, genuine listening skills, be a talented group facilitator and ensure the fact that the plan being developed is done "with" and not "for" the person.

Finally, it is important that champions be positive in their attitude and interactions. As Shawn Achor has suggested, champions should be "praise providers,"[23] **those who seek to bring together people "who bring out the best in others, not the stress in others."[24]**

The term "champion" was deliberately selected to describe the role of the person who has the lead in helping people receiving supports realize their goals because they need to be an inspired advocate, promoter, defender and battler. These individuals should also be optimistic and believe that the next best thing can be achieved. They also need to have grit—the ability to sustain effort in difficult circumstances. Likewise, champions need to have sufficient knowledge of the system they are working in so that they can function successfully within it, but also around it, if necessary. A bit of good advice to those working in bureaucracies is, *"Never accept a 'no' from a person who can't also say 'yes.'"*

The fact is that **people with the qualities to be true champions do exist and are frequently carrying out a personal calling in their lives by helping others.** It is because of their presence that so many lives have been enriched by providers across the country.

Among the many skills needed to carry out plans successfully and help individuals realize their hopes and desires for the future are:

- Clearly knowing and understanding the goal to be pursued
- Identifying the steps to carry out the goal
- Planning strategically, and identifying potential options and alternatives
- Being aware of the challenges, obstacles and resources available
- Knowing not to go with the first solution that solves a problem but working to identify the best solution
- Prioritizing the needed actions
- Identifying allies or those individuals whose help is needed to achieve a goal
- Having more than a "Plan A" when working with more complex goals
- Maintaining a meaningful implementation log for each person served
- Tracking progress, perhaps using an implementation log
- Modifying the plan as necessary.

champion

"YOU'VE
GOT
THIS!"

The Work of a Champion: A Brief Case Study

"To the world, you may
  only be one person, but to
  one person, you may be
  the world."
—Unknown

Malinda Thomas began working at Silverton Community Services, an agency serving people with intellectual and developmental disabilities, three years ago, directly after her graduation from college. She was a psychology major with a minor in English. While she had taken general psychology courses, she had no class work that prepared her to work with people with disabilities.

In terms of life experiences, she had a cousin with Down Syndrome, was aware of high school special education classes, but did not have many opportunities to interact with people with disabilities while growing up. In fact, she wasn't really sure about the differences between people described as mentally ill, or intellectually or cognitively impaired. In spite of her lack of experience, she took the job at Silverton because she wanted to help others, liked people, did not want to go to graduate school, and had heard from friends that Silverton was a good place to work.

After accepting a case manager (QIDP) position at Silverton, Malinda completed the required state training, a combination of classroom and on-the-job learning. She received further in-service training in the basics of behavior analysis, data collection, person-centered planning, survey readiness and communication skills. Since then, she has on occasion been able to attend seminars and webinars that assist her in working with the people that she supports.

What was most helpful was being given a mentor, an experienced and supportive staff member to whom she can turn in matters related to her professional role. Her immediate supervisor, the residential director, is also encouraging and a valuable resource.

Malinda has 18 individuals with a wide range of abilities on her case load. She works two evenings a week from 1:00 to 9:30 p.m., so that she can spend time with the people she supports when they are not at their jobs, in school or attending day programs. She takes advantage of the time and frequently enjoys going out to dinner with them in the evening.

Currently, she is working with Doug Blanchard, a young man in his mid-twenties. He is living with five other men and working 12 hours a week at the Heights Tire Co.

Malinda recently chaired Doug's annual person-centered planning meeting. Doug had invited his mom and dad; Jerry, his job coach; Mary, a direct support staff worker from his home; Jack, a close friend; and Don, a group leader from the church he attends, to join him for the event.

In preparing for the meeting, Malinda talked with Doug about the elements of well-being, making sure he understood the concept as well as he could. Fortunately, he had been able to attend some classes on well-being at the agency. From this conversation, it was clear that Doug wanted to live in an apartment with only one or two roommates—hopefully, his best buddy Jack and maybe Isaac. He also expressed the desire to have a girlfriend and wanted to learn how to dance better. In addition, Doug shared the fact that he was frequently bored since he only worked 12 hours a week.

When Malinda had reviewed the recently completed Personal Outcome Interview with him before the meeting, the responses mirrored their previous conversation except that the health findings revealed more significant difficulties with respect to his vision problems.

Malinda shared the conversation she and Doug had had with the group during the planning meeting with Doug's approval. A fruitful dialogue unfolded, and Doug even talked about his desire to go to the new Star Wars Park in Florida. During the discussion, Doug's mom and dad agreed to take him to his ophthalmologist in the near future, and Jack underscored the fact that he and Doug wanted to live together. Mary, the direct support staff, reminded Doug that he might have to take more frequent showers if he wanted to have a girlfriend and suggested that he also take a class in dating and social etiquette. Don, the church group leader, said he would check to see if there were any volunteer opportunities at the church.

Finally, it was time to get more specific with respect to his "My Plan to Flourish." Doug shared the Personal Profile (part of the plan) that he and Malinda had completed for the meeting. He was very proud of what he and Malinda had put together, and talked at length about gratefulness. All that was needed was to develop the goals and specific goal cards that reflected details and the projected timeframes.

Before turning to that activity, Malinda asked Doug and the group if they thought any new experience might be fun, interesting or helpful to him. Doug didn't think so, but everybody else did—an immediate dilemma. Ideas from the group ranged from offering Doug opportunities to broaden his favorite food repertoire from one—pizza—to other additional selections, such as Chinese. Because Doug had shared his concerns regarding boredom, many suggested hobbies were identified—learning how to fish, woodworking projects and gardening, among many others. Mom and Dad thought Doug should join the YMCA and learn how to swim. No decision was reached, but Malinda and Doug agreed that they would talk some more and even explore other hobby possibilities.

Malinda shared the time span of the goal cards with the group and assisted Doug in prioritizing what he wanted to accomplish. Certain members of the group volunteered to help Doug in accomplishing his goals. This was noted on the cards. Once all of the targeted areas were identified, Doug asked Malinda to write them down because of his limited writing ability.

Malinda and Doug would now work out the details and steps to accomplish the goals. Here are the goals they listed:

Near-Term (From the Present to One Year)

1. Doug developed a goal that he and Jack would spend more time together—at least one day each weekend.
2. Doug would like to learn more about the Star Wars Park in Florida to see if he could afford to visit it.
3. Doug wants to learn how to dance better and would like Malinda to help him identify learning opportunities and other possible hobbies, so he can be more active and less bored.

4. An appointment with the ophthalmologist is needed for Doug to ensure optimal eye health. His parents are working to make the appointment and will take him to the office.
5. Doug plans to work with Malinda and apply for a housing voucher since it takes a long time for approval.

Mid-Term (Two to Four Years)

1. Doug hopes to have a serious girlfriend within a few years. His support team will help him come up with a game plan to go forward.
2. Doug plans to move into an affordable apartment with Jack within the next two years. However, Jack is having major surgery in a few months, and Doug needs to save for the deposit on an apartment.

Long-Term (Many Years)

1. Doug shared his desire to be able to read comic books. Given Doug's significant vision impairment, he is seeking the advice of his ophthalmologist. He and his family will plan accordingly.
2. Doug would like to find a job as a mechanic. Someday, he would also like to be married.

Goals Suggested by Others

1. After discussing dating and having a girlfriend, Doug agreed to follow the advice of his support team and shower at least three times a week.
2. Doug liked the idea of going shopping with his mom and dad to buy some new clothes.
3. Doug is going to talk to his boss at Heights Tire about the possibility of working additional hours.

Malinda finished writing out the goals and handed them to Doug. He took the cards and placed them inside his "Plan to Flourish." He also thanked his friends and family for attending the meeting. Malinda then asked Doug if he wanted to end the meeting, which he did. As everyone gathered their belongings and prepared to leave, Malinda thanked everyone for their support, and told them that she would continue to meet with Doug to review his progress and identify any assistance he might need to accomplish his goals.

The Personal Sketch

One of Silverton Community Services' communication practices includes sharing a personal sketch describing each person supported in their residential and day programs. This information introduces the people receiving support to the staff working with them and is especially useful to new staff members.

A sketch introduces the person in an in-depth, personal way. Nowhere is the use of humanizing language as important as it is in this section of the plan. The standard is to describe people as we would like to be described. To allow language that is pejorative is to continue to allow less than what we would want for ourselves.[25]

The personal sketch provides helpful insights and observations that assist staff members in creating a mental image of the person. They should, after reading the material, be able to pick the person out of a crowd. Readers would know something of his appearance and how he presents himself to the world. They could tell someone else about his interests and hobbies—perhaps he has a favorite expression or style of clothing.[26]

Personal sketches are completed and updated as appropriate or as part of the annual person-centered review process. Efforts are made to limit the "Personal Sketch" to one page. Doug Blanchard's "Personal Sketch" follows.

Personal Sketch: Doug Blanchard

Doug Blanchard (created identity) is a slender, five-foot, ten-inch, 24-year-old man. While his proper name is Douglas, he really prefers being called Doug. He enjoys sports, especially basketball and soccer, and riding his bike with his friends. Except for a chronic eye disorder that sometimes results in cloudy vision and the need for eye drops, and a heart condition, Doug is in good health.

Doug likes people and gets along well with others. He likes to be helpful around others and volunteers to take out the garbage, do household chores and be in charge of his home's recycling—he takes the recycling materials out to the curb every two weeks. However, he becomes upset when housemates or friends get into arguments. Yelling upsets Doug.

He enjoys putting together Lego kits and saves money from his job at Heights Tire to buy them. He is very proud of his job, likes his coworkers and always gets to work on time.

Doug's best friend is Jack, although he also likes to hang out with another friend, Isaac. They hope to live together in an apartment in the future. Currently, they are working on plans to make that possible. Doug lets everyone know he is going to buy a Roomba—he likes robots—to clean the floors of their apartment. He also wants to learn how to cook more "dishes" for himself and his friends. Doug's dad is teaching him how to use a small backyard barbeque grill.

Doug also likes to watch space movies on TV, especially *Star Wars* and *Star Trek*. He would like to go to the new Disneyland Park, Star Wars Galaxy's Edge, in Florida.

CHAPTER 8

My Plan to Flourish: What It's All About

> "The sooner you start planning your life, the sooner you will live the life you dream of."
>
> —Hans Glint

We have finally come to the heart of this book, crafting a person-centered plan for a person who needs supports in living. Hopefully, the reader has come to understand and appreciate one of the major tenets presented here—we can live a better life if we want to. In fact, we human beings are either getting better or worse. We don't stay the same. Likewise, we are either going forward or backward, and setting goals offers us one of the most effective ways to move forward.

The Components of "My Plan to Flourish"

"My Plan to Flourish" essentially consists of two components:

The Personal Profile

1. A trifold with the name of the person printed on its cover.

The cover and the five additional panels provide eight
Communication Channels:

- I Am Grateful—panel 1 (cover)
- What People Like and Admire About Me—panel 2
- Keys to Coaching Me—panel 3
- What Makes Me Uncomfortable—panel 3
- I Am Proud Of—panel 4
- Health and Wellness—panel 5
- My Priorities—panel 6
- My Interests—panel 6

Goals

2. A set of goal cards.

The number of cards will depend on the person but generally
follow the sequence of:

- Near-Term (From the Present to One Year)
- Mid-Term (Two to Four Years)
- Long-Term (Many Years)
- Goals Suggested by Others.

Plan Description: The Personal Profile

The actual "My Plan to Flourish" is an 8½" × 11" sheet of cardstock, presented as a trifold and printed with the fields listed above. The goal cards are 3" × 8½" and are also created on light cardstock; both sides can be used. They can be inserted inside the trifold, which is then placed in a 4" × 9½" envelope. (See the accompanying illustration.) The plan packet was designed to be easily accessible to the person and those who support him.

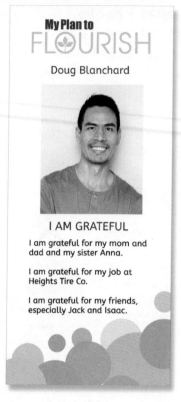

My Plan to
FL◉URISH

Doug Blanchard

I AM GRATEFUL

I am grateful for my mom and dad and my sister Anna.

I am grateful for my job at Heights Tire Co.

I am grateful for my friends, especially Jack and Isaac.

Panel 1: The Cover

When putting the "My Plan to Flourish" plan together from a visual perspective, it is important to create an attractive graphic design. In the example being presented, you will note that there are opportunities to include a graphic or picture that further communicates the personality of the person in terms of interests or experiences.

The top of the page should have the person's full name. If the person prefers a first "nickname" rather than a legal name, it should be used.

A high quality picture should appear below the name—at least 2 ½ inches square. Ideally, the picture shows the person in a setting of his choice. It should not be a mug shot. It's also important to place photos in the document so that there is no distortion. This may require getting assistance from someone who has experience editing and sizing photos successfully.

Below the picture on the cover is the first heading: "I Am Grateful." As discussed previously, a spirit of gratitude leads to positive emotions. This approach also introduces the person to others on the basis of seeking to create a positive relationship. Gratitude makes life more satisfying for the person, and allows him to share and remember positive thoughts and experiences.

Panel 2: What People Like and Admire About Me

This section is an extension of the positive introduction that is not only important to the person in the context of PERMAH and his desire to flourish, but also to those who may be sought to assist him with his goals.

There is room on this page for several positive and uplifting statements. The intent is to have three to five sentences with space in between, so the reader can easily determine the statement distinctions. It should not take on the appearance of a newspaper column. As Lady Mary Montagu observed many years ago, "You can be pleased with nothing when you are not pleased with yourself."

Note the use of the first person (I, me and my). This is not meant to replace the usefulness of having a personal sketch narrative. Indeed, that should be available in the "Person-Centered Record," and easily accessible to direct support staff in a person's day program or residence if he is living in a staff-supported residence.

WHAT PEOPLE LIKE AND ADMIRE ABOUT ME

I like helping people, running errands and walking our family dog, Brutus.

I have had a job for over five years and I never miss work, and I am always on time.

I am easy going and get along with my housemates.

I am good at grocery shopping. I like picking out things, especially fruit.

Panel 3: Keys to Coaching Me

This section is designed to inform the individuals working most closely with the person as they help him carry out the key elements of support. What should be included? What works best for him in terms of encouragement, redirecting when necessary, and noting any unusual behaviors that occur and the circumstances under which those behaviors take place. Communication and language topics could also be included.

In addition, it could encompass instances when a person clearly prefers to be called Harold rather than Harry, for example. Some individuals do not wish to be touched, so friendly pats on the shoulder should not be used. Others that we support may be very sensitive to the sound of loud noises, so our "outdoor voice" would clearly be inappropriate.

The focus of this section is on giving a staff member or employer, for example, simple tools to help the person if any rough spots are encountered, and ideally to prevent problems. Examples of content might include key phrases that the person finds calming, or key phrases/ topics to avoid using when talking to him. Suggestions for effective ways to inform the person about unavoidable schedule changes, for instance, might be critical for some. Another person might be frightened by severe weather and need special support during those times.

KEYS TO COACHING ME

I do not like it when people yell at each other or at me.

Sometimes I learn better when people show me how to do something instead of just telling me.

I like to be called Doug, not Douglass.

When I am deciding things I like to take my time and not be rushed.

WHAT MAKES ME UNCOMFORTABLE

I don't like it when people have arguments or are bossy.

I get worried when I don't hear from my dad or mom.

Video games that are too hard for me to play.

I don't like riding in a van especially the last seat.

Going to a new restaurant.

The point is to draw attention to any critical needs the person might have that are likely to occur during the course of a significant inter-action with him, or are so severe that a staff member must know how to address them.

This is not meant to be the conveyance of a complex behavior support plan; however. If there is such a plan, reference it in this sec-tion by adding, "For more information about coaching me, see my Personal Record." We suggest that support staff read this plan prior to working directly in a one-to-one relationship with the person. That said, it is not necessary for everyone seeking to assist people who require supports to know everything about everybody.

Panel 3: What Makes Me Uncomfortable

This space can be adjusted with the "Keys to Coaching Me" section above. As may be anticipated, the information it contains is highly variable, given the person receiving support, and may be as vanilla as, "I don't like it when someone tells me they are a Chicago White Sox fan." For others, however, this is an important inclusion and may deal with serious behavior challenges, including aggression or self-injurious behavior.

Again, its purpose is to communi-cate the most significant variables and emphasize the nature of the most appropriate response. Referring the reader to the Personal Record may also be apropos in this section.

KEYS TO COACHING ME

I do not like it when people yell at each other or at me.

Sometimes I learn better when people show me how to do something instead of just telling me.

I like to be called Doug, not Douglass.

When I am deciding things I like to take my time and not be rushed.

WHAT MAKES ME UNCOMFORTABLE

I don't like it when people have arguments or are bossy.

I get worried when I don't hear from my dad or mom.

Video games that are too hard for me to play.

I don't like riding in a van especially the last seat.

Going to a new restaurant.

Panel 4: I Am Proud Of

Once again, the purpose is to introduce the person in a manner that facilitates social interaction and a sense of worth. Included in this section could be recent accomplishments, possessions and lifestyle changes:

- "I have a new job."
- "I am going to a new church."
- "I joined the Model Railroad Club."

There may be the opportunity for a photo in this section as well.

> **I AM PROUD OF**
>
> I am proud of the things I have bought with my paycheck, like my favorite space movies, posters and slingshot.
>
> I am proud of the buildings I have made with my Lego Set.
>
> I have been the "employee of the month" at Heights Tire Co.
>
> I can make grilled cheese sandwiches, and make a fire outside to cook hotdogs and roast marshmallows.
>
> I can read a little bit better than last year.
>
> *A New Plan* Copyright 2020 High Tide Press

Panel 5: Health and Wellness

It is well known that persons with disabilities are prone to more health problems than others. Health, therefore, is a very important consideration in providing them with effective supports. While this is a fact, the premise is that not everyone needs to know everything. For example, that a person had prostate cancer five years ago has no bearing on helping him get a job today. On the other hand, this is important information to have in the medical section of a Personal Record, just not in a person's "My Plan to Flourish."

> **HEALTH & WELLNESS**
>
> I have bad allergies to grasses and things that make me sneeze like cottonwood trees.
>
> I can't eat strawberries or pineapples.
>
> Sometimes I have problems seeing clearly and have to have drops in my eyes. My medical chart has the details of my eye problems.
>
> I like sports, especially basketball and soccer. I also like riding my bike with my friends on the bike trails.
>
> My doctor told me I was doing good.

Likewise, if a person is taking medication for depression and not experiencing any side effects or expressing any concerns, such information does not need to be noted in the section. If, on the other hand, the person has a significant, secondary diagnosis of mental illness that may be impairing his performance, an appropriate notation might read, "Currently, I am taking medication for a psychiatric illness. Information regarding my treatment can be found in the health/medical section of my Personal Record."

It may be very important, however, to communicate those factors that have a bearing on current supports, such as having a swallowing disorder, a pacemaker, frequent seizures, gait unsteadiness, or other conditions. In these cases, referring the reader to the person's health record may be in order.

Panel 6: My Priorities

This section is designed to reflect the person's general priorities with respect to his life planning—not an exhaustive list of favorite colors or TV programs. Such things as spending time with a certain friend, getting a job, visiting a particular park, saving for a new item and trying something new are typical entries.

Panel 6: My Interests

This section can often be lengthy— which is a good thing. As a result, bullet points can be used. The list may include hobbies, church attendance, sports teams, physical exercise, such as "riding my bike," certain TV programs, and favorite restaurants, among others.

MY PRIORITIES

I like going out to eat, especially getting pizza.

I would like to spend more time with my buddies, Jack and Isaac. We would like to live together in our own apartment.

I would like to learn how to cook more foods.

MY INTERESTS

* Building Lego kits
* Star Wars and space movies
* Going out to eat
* Playing sports, bike riding
* Going to church with Mom and Dad
* Cooking
* Having friends
* Doing good at my job
* Watching rodeos on T.V.

-Doug Blanchard- 2020

Plan Description: Goals

Understanding Goals

An essential element of the "My Plan to Flourish" is the recognition that we human beings all want to reach a desired end or outcome. We call these desired end states goals, future accomplishments that take time to achieve. Some of the things we seek can be accomplished through little effort in relatively short periods of time, while others may be understood as hopes or dreams that represent a lifelong commitment requiring much effort. Interestingly, written goals provide the most motivation, especially when they are meaningful, and reflect thoughtful decision making and choice selection.

As suggested earlier, goals should neither be too hard nor too easy. In fact, higher goals—for example, seeking to graduate from college—require a higher level of effort and commitment. In a similar manner, goals should be prioritized and tracked according to our intrinsic motivation. Therefore, having too many goals may ensure that we achieve none of them. As Seth Godin has observed, **"The person who invented the ship, also invented the shipwreck."**[27]

Later in this chapter, we discuss the nature of hopes and dreams. These more general goals can certainly be included or identified in one's "My Plan to Flourish" without having steps, specific dates or measurable outcomes. Some people, for example, may believe that they "should probably lose some weight, but now is not the time" for any number of reasons. They might include current stress or health-related limitations, such as taking medications that induce weight gain. But it still may be important to write the desired outcome down. It better locks the desire into our internal motivation system. Such an approach allows us to be self-energizing without lowering our self-esteem.

Written goals provide the most motivation.

Intrinsic vs. Extrinsic Goals

While opinions differ, goals are characterized as being intrinsic or extrinsic. Identifying very personal goals would be considered intrinsic. They include things we want for ourselves, such as weight loss or elective surgery. Intrinsic goals reflect the self-attitude of "I want to…" rather than the burden of "I have to…."

Extrinsic goals, on the other hand, generally emerge with respect to others and our desire to please or impact them. Such goals could involve gaining a specific membership to a club to impress our coworkers; joining and participating in Special Olympics to make our moms and dads happy; or leaving a job we like because our significant others want us to work at the place where they are employed. It is not uncommon, in fact, that pursuing such goals actually backfires and can lower our self-esteem.

Positive Goals

It is important in person-centered planning to **emphasize positive "approach goals" rather than negative "avoidance" ones.** As Caroline Webb states in *How to Have a Good Day,* "If we want to boost our chances of success, research suggests that we should aim to describe [our goals] in a way that is positive, personally meaningful, feasible and situation-specific."[28]

In some research studies, setting avoidance goals, such as, "I do not want to be tardy any more going to work," can actually hurt performance. It is much better to reframe the goal from the perspective of positive performance—"I would like to…."

Modifying Goals

There are times when it may be important to change a goal or modify it, and that is because singular devotion to one goal in terms of time and effort may actually cancel out or preclude the attainment of other important goals. For example, if a person is working in a subminimal job situation and sets a goal of making more money, he might be able to do so. However, if he doesn't even like the job, he may be miserable while making more money. What he should really do is move on and find better employment. This, again, is why having a support group, or if not that, a champion—perhaps a possibility trainer—is important. There is someone to talk to and help the person think through his goals.

Another good reason to seek the assistance of others (a support team) is that it provides a person the opportunity to ask for their feed-back on goals to ensure they are right for him. He may desire a certain end, but if it were attained, his situation might, in fact, be worse as a result. For example, a woman might want to live with or marry a "friend" who is exploiting her for her money because of drug addiction. **Life satisfaction isn't just about setting goals. It's also about having goals congruent with a positive and constructive life.**

As desirable as it is to have a small group of supporters and advisors, it is wise to be aware of the possible presence of "planning fallacies." This occurs, for instance, when a group of people working together underestimate the costs, time to complete and risks of a particular pursuit—goal—or overestimate the benefits and lasting value to the person. Sometimes it happens because of their own wishful thinking— they want what's best for the person they support, but don't take time to think through all of the things in his life that change.

Developing Goals

Writing goals down also serves as a reminder to coach ourselves when we are ready. A good way to do so is to use the GROW model.[29]

Developed originally for coaching athletes, it has been applied in a variety of contexts because it is a simple, adaptable tool. Since it lends itself well to the planning process, it can be modified without great difficulty to help people with disabilities develop their personal plans. Of course, the staff member (champion) or family member, who takes the place of a coach, must remember throughout the process that he is a guide and the person with the disability is the one making the decisions. The acrostic provides users with an easy way to remember the steps in the process:

G—Setting the *goal*

The first step addresses the question, "**What do I want to accomplish?**" The person's coach or champion should help him explore identified desires for both the short-term and long-term future by asking questions, such as:

- **What do you enjoy doing?** (Make a list of those activities.)
- **Is there something you would like to learn or accomplish related to that or those activities?** (Make a list of those goals. They should be specific, clear and reasonable, given the abilities the person planning has.)
- **Which goals do you feel excited about?** (This question might help pare down a long list or modify a goal to make it more motivating. The person creating the plan will not stick with what is required to achieve the goal(s) unless there is positive emotional investment.)
- **How will the goals you are choosing make your life better?** (Identify the benefits that will result from achieving the goal. For instance, if the planner wishes to learn to cook a particular dish, he may say:
  - "It's fun to cook new dishes."
  - "It tastes very good."
  - "It is more nutritious than most of the things I eat."
  - "My friends really like it.")

- **How many goals should you set?** (The cardinal guide is how many goals does the person think he can effectively tackle. Generally speaking, it is best to limit goals to no more than two or three per time period you set. [See the discussion of time and goals later in this chapter.] Too many goals ensure that the person will not accomplish much at all. Since "My Plan to Flourish" is to be reviewed and adjusted regularly, the goals can be revised should the person change his mind about any one of them.)

R—Doing a *reality* check

The second step requires answering the question, **"What are the current realities I face in relation to the goal?"** The person planning must consider the facts of his life and abilities rather than engage in wishful thinking. Some questions he might ask are:

- **Where are you now in relation to the goal?** (This requires assessing whether the person planning knows anything about the activity and if so, how much.)
- **Do you have the resources you need to accomplish the goal?** (Taking stock of resources might include considering the money required for a trip to the Grand Canyon, or the strength expected of someone who wishes to run or walk a 5K, along with access to a place to train.)
- **What are the obstacles?** (While obstacles may include things that make the goal impossible, they may simply make attaining it difficult. Knowing exactly what the problems are will help the person assess his ability to overcome them.)

O—Considering possible *options*

The third step asks the planner to think about the question, **"What courses of action could I take or strategies could I use to accomplish my goal?"** The option step offers the person the opportunity to out-line some things he might use to achieve the goals under consideration. It also allows for modifying them if the obstacles to accomplishing them seem insurmountable. The following questions are a few one might think through.

- **What are some steps you can take to get to the goal?** (This question requires the planner to brainstorm and write down steps that seem to advance him toward the goal in question.)
- **Which ones are things you can do or have someone help you do?** (In this case, the person creating the plan makes an honest assessment. Questions might include:
  - What makes me believe that I can accomplish this step on my own?
  - Why do I need help on this particular step?
  - What kind of help is available to me?)

W—Assessing *what* actions to take that *will* actually achieve the goal

After considering the options, it is time to outline the steps necessary to accomplish each goal. The person developing his plan might summarize what was learned through the options process by answering the question, **"Do I have a clear understanding of what is to be done and what it takes to achieve the goal?"** When the answer is, "Yes," he can begin going through the list of goals that have been compiled and develop the steps required to achieve them. He should ask the following questions as he considers each goal.

- **Is the goal sufficiently specific?** (The person should make a final assessment of the goal, ensuring that it is not too broad and states exactly what he wants to achieve.)
- **What steps will you follow to get there?** (Answering this question takes some time since each goal must have clear, reasonable steps that state exactly what the planner needs to do at each point. It also makes tracking progress easier.)

Too many goals ensure that the person will not accomplish much at all.

- **How long will it take?** (Time estimates will, of course, be just that—estimates. They may need to be revised at regular intervals. If the revisions lengthen the time needed to achieve the goal, it should not be regarded as failure. No one can know every obstacle that might interfere with the process.)
- **What will you look/feel like when you get to the "finish line"?** (Keeping a clear picture of how achieving the goal will affect the person is highly motivating. The picture can be mental or, when appropriate, visually depicted so that it is never forgotten.)

The Approach

At this point, we will assume that the champion (facilitator), who serves as the chair of the person-centered planning process, has a relationship with the person receiving supports and has discussed and shown him what the plan will look like. As a result, the person hopefully understands the intent of all of the elements. Likewise, the other individuals attending the planning meetings—family, friends and staff— need to be familiar with the "My Plan to Flourish" approach, at least in general terms. It might also help to send an overview of the positive planning approach to attendees in advance. In addition, they should understand that the planning process is ongoing and may take several meetings to develop a meaningful plan.

Depending on the person, many of the eight elements shared in the trifold could quite possibly be completed before the goal-setting session and may also be clarified, or added to, during the meeting. Obviously, the process and plan development will be different for a person brand new to services and supports than for a person who has been supported by an agency for a number of years.

We recommend that providers using this approach offer classes and learning experiences for those they serve in the six elements of well-being as well as other relevant topics, such as gratitude, and identifying values and preferences. In ideal circumstances, the person receiving supports will have been engaged in enough background work that he knows goal setting is important and involves some measure of self-examination and personal inventory that answers the question, "What do I have in stock?" They will know that goals take effort and time to fulfill. It may also be helpful to offer the person who is setting goals and the other attendees a review of the 21 Personal Outcome Measures®, developed by the CQL, in preparation for a plan development meeting.

My Plan to Flourish

Generally speaking, goals developed using the "My Plan to Flourish" approach are identified across three time periods (though these are not rigid): from months to approximately one year, from two to four years; and finally those that may be five years or more. Also included is a fourth goal area labeled, "Goals Suggested by Others." This is an optional goal category that can be selected and developed if so desired and promote, for example, a person's health or safety. This goal category may be of particular importance for individuals with complex needs or challenging behavior.

Movement toward goal accomplishment occurs through regular tracking and monitoring. We suggest that this occur on a monthly basis for near-term goals and any others that may be accomplished in a shorter period of time. It is also important to track mid-term and long-term goals by month to identify noteworthy progress toward achieving them. Tracking long-term goals by month may seem unnecessary, but the regular review keeps them in mind and encourages the person to keep working toward the desired end. From a practical perspective, it is advisable to prioritize the goals in each of the three time dimensions. The fourth may include only one or two goals.

Tier I: Near-Term (From the Present to One Year)
This goal area may be the least complicated; therefore, the targeted goals might not require support with many specific steps. Accomplishment is often a function of enabling resources and proper timing. However, these goals are not "to-do lists." They, like all goals, require personal effort to achieve them.

> Doug and Jack will spend more time together-at least one day each weekend.
>
> Doug would like to learn more about the Star Wars park in Florida to see if he could afford to visit it.
>
> Doug wants to learn how to dance better and would like Malinda to help him identify learning opportunities and other possible hobbies so he can be more active and less bored.
>
> An appointment to the opthalmologist is needed for Doug to ensure optimal eye health. His parents are working to make the appointment and will take him to the office.
>
> Doug plans to work with Malinda and apply for a housing voucher since it takes a long time for approval.

**1.
Near-Term**

Tier 2: Mid-Term (Two to Four Years)
This tier can be the busiest in terms of planning, setting goals and re-adjusting or recalibrating them. Likewise, it can include goals that are not rapidly changing because of the learning that may need to occur in the process of achievement. It is also likely that many of those desired goals will require a substructure for completion—specific steps that lead to the goals.

> Doug hopes to have a serious girlfriend within a few years. His support team will help him come up with a game plan to go forward.
>
> Doug plans to move into an affordable apartment with Jack within the next two years. However, Jack is having major surgery in a few months and Doug needs to save for the deposit on an apartment.

**2.
Mid-Term**

Tier 3: Long-Term (Many Years)

This timeframe is often described as the hopes and dreams a person has for his life, friends or closest relationships, and/or for his home, work or retirement. It can also reflect significant educational or vocational goals.

It is not unusual for these goals to change over time, whether because of experiences, friendships, health or personal finances. By having such long-term goals, a person is more likely to act positively toward the future rather than just accepting what comes his way.

Long-term goals might have to be inferred for those people who have very limited cognitive abilities. Often, those who know the person best, such as family members and support staff, will have ideas and suggestions for this area. A good place to start is with relationships. Does he feel better in the company of family, friends or other valued connections? What helps him be involved with his environment? In other words, think in terms of his flourishing vs. languishing. Remember, you're helping the person develop his dreams. What could those be?

> **3.**
> **Long-Term**
>
> Doug shared his desire to be able to read comic books. Given Doug's significant vision impairment, he is seeking the advice of his opthalmologist. He and his family will plan accordingly.
>
> Doug would like to find a job as a mechanic. Someday, he would also like to be married.

Tier 4: Goals Suggested by Others

It's a fact of life that many goals that we ultimately select for ourselves may have been recommended by others. Health is a prime example. Often, physicians or other medical specialists will recommend medications or lifestyle changes. Recommended goals may also come from family, friends, counselors, life coaches or support teams. The time-frames can span all three tiers.

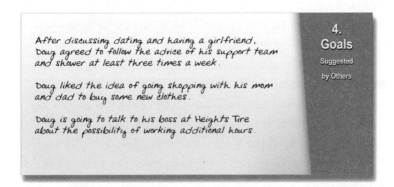

After discussing dating and having a girlfriend, Doug agreed to follow the advice of his support team and shower at least three times a week.

Doug liked the idea of going shopping with his mom and dad to buy some new clothes.

Doug is going to talk to his boss at Heights Tire about the possibility of working additional hours.

4.
Goals
Suggested
by Others

Using the Goal Cards

Goal cards are an integral part of every Flourish Plan. They are filled out to reflect each tier and then kept inside a person's plan envelope. The cards for goals, modified as a result of progress or other revisions, are discarded and new cards developed to replace them.

For some individuals with greater reading ability, the cards will do quite well and accomplish their purpose. If possible, the person, whose plan it is, should jot down his goals in his own printing or handwriting—with assistance if necessary. Research has established that writing our goals down helps the brain encode the message. In that case, the goal cards would be written in the first person ("I would like to…."). When the cards need to be written for him, it is fine to write them in the third person ("Doug would like to….").

For others, the cards may need to be made more interactive in an effort to encourage the individuals to value and act on them. It really doesn't make any difference how many cards are used to communicate a goal. There is no rule that only four cards are the limit. For example, the person for whom the plan is crafted may want to go fishing for a day in a boat out on a lake. He can't say that or read it, but with some help can tape or glue two or three pictures to one card or more and know what it refers to. The goal could be typed or written on the reverse side to minimize any misunderstanding.

Involving as many of the senses as possible always aids memory and engagement. Some of the same strategies that would help someone without disabilities keep track of goal progress might be helpful to someone with a disability. These might include things like checklists, phone-based reminder programs, notebooks to record progress, inspirational posters or pictures, and planning what kind of celebration will happen when a step is achieved.

1.
Near Term

I want to go fishing at least one time this summer.
I would like to catch fish at Lake Nokoma.
I plan to rent a boat at the lake for fishing in July or August.
I will ask my friend, Jeff, if he would like to go with me.

People who have health-related goals often use fitness apps to track everything from their biometric measures to the number of steps they have walked/run. Personal fitness devices support people without disabilities every day, and there are simplified apps designed for fitness novices or young people that can be adapted for people with disabilities.

Still others who wish to personalize their goals but cannot write may benefit from using a signature stamp to record their names on the cards. These personal stamps can be developed by:

- **Having two or three staff members write the person's name and allow him to choose the most appealing style.**
- **Guiding the person's hand in writing his name.**
- **Having the person place his hand on a staff member's hand and write his name.**[30]

Finally, when a person achieves a significant goal, a celebration is in order. Goals achieved could be celebrated on a brightly colored card that would also be included in the card envelope. It could have words or pictures/symbols that depict the accomplishment.

The Importance of Action Steps

It is important in supporting a person who's crafting his "My Plan to Flourish" to remember that it is his plan, and the person himself should play the pivotal role in advancing his goals to the greatest extent possible. This naturally means taking on more responsibility than what typically occurs in the development of person-centered plans.

It is a task of the champion and support teams (when available) to determine whether or not sub-goals or action steps might be beneficial in the achievement of outcomes. Long-range or complex goals may benefit from steps as progress toward these milestones might sustain motivation.

Further, two people with the same goals may vary greatly in the number of steps needed to reach the stated goal. As mentioned previously, motivation, skill level or availability of supports also varies by person. For some individuals, the goal of reading is very daunting. For others, it could be dressing themselves or even brushing their teeth. It's also important to recognize that a person with sensory deficits, such as blindness or deafness, may require more steps in skill acquisition than a person without such impediments. When identified, these steps should be pursued in progressive order.

When Goals Are Not Achieved

No one in life achieves all of their goals. Some are failed; some are quit, and quite likely many are simply changed or discarded. We should not be surprised when people change their minds and, when after reflection, new information or experiences, they decide to do something different.

Having a plan and tracking progress is essential to motivation. Therefore, it is important for the champion to be meeting with the person regularly. Dialogue about goal progress needs to be ongoing. When progress stalls or ground is lost along the way, the champion must be prepared to discuss the situation, identify obstacles and determine the current level of commitment to achieving the goal. The discussion may also include suggestions for modifying the plan's timetable or identifying smaller steps that need to be taken to achieve the goal. In addition, it may be helpful to examine the presence of motivational supports, such as friends or posters.

There may be occasions when a person supported simply feels that a goal—for example, pursuing a desire to sing in a specific choir— will likely not be achieved after several "try-outs." What happens next? We recommend that the champion and appropriate persons close to the goal seeker work hard to understand the goal. Does it have a special meaning? Could the person join a less competitive choir? Is there a next best thing, hobby, or other activity that could be pursued? People are much more resilient than we often realize. They may experience a period of anger or discouragement, but it's very probable that another meaningful, achievable goal will be identified.

CHAPTER 9

The Bottom Line: Implementation

> "What you get by achieving your goals is not as important as what you become by achieving your goals."
> —Henry David Thoreau

It does little good to assist a person receiving support in developing a "My Plan to Flourish" if no one acts on it—said another way, if it's not implemented. We have already stated that if a person neither likes her plan nor wants it, the document will not be meaningful. In that case, the plan more likely becomes an exercise in regulatory compliance and something that staff do for people or do to them.

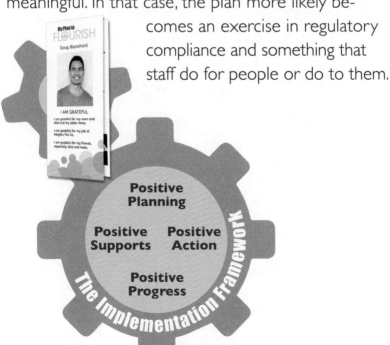

A Framework for Implementation

We have spent considerable time discussing person-centered thinking and planning and, specifically, the crafting of "My Plan to Flourish," so the next step involves developing an implementation strategy that works. The Implementation Framework shown below is designed as a visual and conceptual overview of the model, which highlights its most critical dimensions.

You will note that the "My Plan to Flourish" Implementation Framework rests fully in the Organizational Inventory of Person-Centeredness as outlined in Chapter 10. Together the tools provide a synergistic assessment of the person-centered planning process.

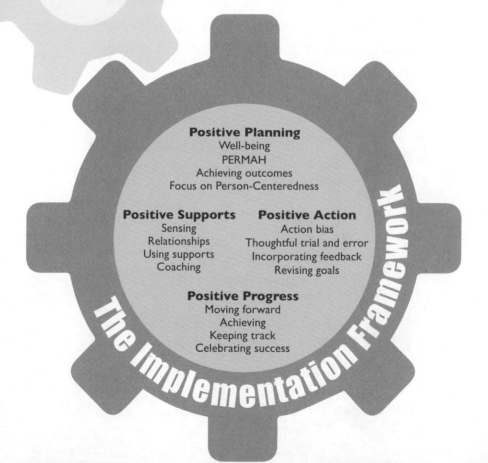

Positive Planning
Well-being
PERMAH
Achieving outcomes
Focus on Person-Centeredness

Positive Supports
Sensing
Relationships
Using supports
Coaching

Positive Action
Action bias
Thoughtful trial and error
Incorporating feedback
Revising goals

Positive Progress
Moving forward
Achieving
Keeping track
Celebrating success

The Implementation Framework

A Guide for Champions

The "My Plan to Flourish" implementation framework is presented as a structure containing the four core dimensions that drive quality person-centered planning.

Positive Planning captures the essence of the plan. The goal is to experience well-being through the feelings and thoughts of positive emotions, engagement, positive relationships, meaning, accomplishment and health. The principles of person-centeredness are acknowledged and followed, and the person being supported experiences her personal outcomes.

Positive Supports emphasizes the personal and people side of the process—from the motivation of the person supported, to family and friends, life coaches, and direct and non-direct support staff. It's founded on the premise that it's with others that we transform ourselves and the world.

Positive Action captures the importance of leadership and energy. It's how we leave our comfort zone and open the doors to change, and begin to explore more and achieve more. Errors are okay and feedback allows for self-correction, and if need be, the revision of goals.

Positive Progress involves quite a bit of self-reflection. The person considers whether forward movement is occurring and progress is being made. It's impossible to determine where you are, how far you've come or how far you can go without measurement. The driver who knows how many miles he gets to a gallon has a clear advantage over the driver who does not. And finally, it's important to celebrate all successes, large and small.

Leadership and energy: It's how we leave our comfort zone and open the doors to change, and begin to explore more and achieve more.

The framework centerpiece aligns the four core dimensions together in an important synergy—the crafting of "My Plan to Flourish." The plan is the "go to" document for recording and communicating the planning that resulted in the identification of future goals. As previously noted, **goal setting is a life-long adventure.**

The framework is primarily directed to champions or those individuals who have made a personal commitment to assist others in living their best life possible. Such individuals are whole-hearted in this endeavor, ardent in their spirit, capable of overcoming obstacles, taking countermeasures when necessary, and emphatic in their actions.

Use this framework to step back and look at your approach. Are you visiting all four dimensions? Are there areas that need to be strengthened? Do you need to increase your knowledge of any of the content areas that would allow you to be more confident or comfortable in your implementation efforts?

Supporting a Person with Intellectual Disabilities

Before discussing implementation further, it may be helpful to review the nature of cognitive impairments as they relate to intellectual disabilities. It is important to remember that such descriptors vary in their character and severity of impact with each person. These limitations should be kept in mind because they affect both the development and implementation of a person-centered plan. Some of them may include:

- Difficulty understanding abstract concepts
- Difficulty understanding complex information
- Length of time required to learn concepts and skills
- Difficulties with memory
- Difficulty with problem solving and goal setting
- Low academic achievement
- Weak social skills
- Poor attention span.

Having a general understanding of these characteristics when supporting an individual with I/DD reduces the chances that there will be major problems in relationship building, communication or performance expectations.

Unfortunately, people in some settings make a strong effort to set aside the reality of limitations and behave as if the individuals receiving support have none. However, knowing that reality and keeping it in mind during the planning process in no way diminishes respect for persons who have a disability. **Not to consider the limitations is, in fact, unfair to and hampers the process of helping people set goals and live their best life possible.**

The Obstacles to Plan Implementation and a Fulfilled Life

Part of being human is to be aware that we will confront obstacles every day in whatever we pursue. That's no big news. What makes the difference is how we think about the obstacles and what we do about them. So it is with those who seek to assist and support people in carrying out their "Plan to Flourish." Obstacles will arise, and we must work to overcome them.

Before considering some of the external obstacles and systems problems in implementation, it may prove helpful to examine some of the obstacles we create for ourselves.

A Compliance Mindset

It is apparent that some staff members have been beaten down by the regulatory environment and still others by a negative, energy-zapping organizational culture. Not surprisingly, they evidence the characteristics of learned helplessness.

Note to the Risk Averse: It is quite likely that many readers will say, "The 'My Plan to Flourish' is nice, but we can't use it. Our state, county or organization requires us to follow the plan directed by the regulations." That, of course, is why plans become 20 or more pages in length. It's as if the best plan is the longest one. This occurs in large part because of federal guidelines that state that nearly everything, including a description of the kitchen sink, should be in the plan.

As stated earlier, providers need to collect a great deal of information essential to supporting a person and have it accessible. That information, however, does not need to be in a person's plan for the future. It should instead be a part of a person-centered "record." Federal and state regulations need to be changed to recognize the distinction. This makes sense because, with the celebration of increased computerization of assessments, comes the realization that the actual result may be printouts that become an obstacle to person-centered planning rather than a help. They contain so much background information, sometimes useless federal requirements, and items to be included from dropdown boxes that the person's needs, wants and hopes have been hidden under a bushel, and the "light" has been going out.

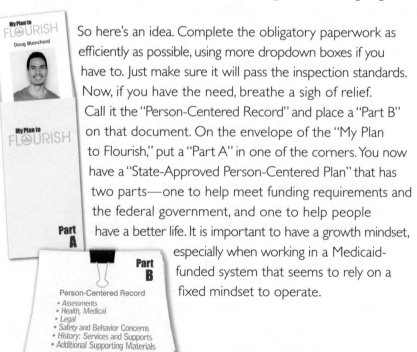

So here's an idea. Complete the obligatory paperwork as efficiently as possible, using more dropdown boxes if you have to. Just make sure it will pass the inspection standards. Now, if you have the need, breathe a sigh of relief. Call it the "Person-Centered Record" and place a "Part B" on that document. On the envelope of the "My Plan to Flourish," put a "Part A" in one of the corners. You now have a "State-Approved Person-Centered Plan" that has two parts—one to help meet funding requirements and the federal government, and one to help people have a better life. It is important to have a growth mindset, especially when working in a Medicaid-funded system that seems to rely on a fixed mindset to operate.

Understanding the Essence
of Person-Centered Thinking and Planning

In a college class, one of the authors had a professor who assigned a difficult book to read as a class assignment. When called upon, one student struggled to explain the primary themes. At that point, the professor remarked, "It is clear you have gone through the book, but the book hasn't gone through you." So it is with many people who work at person-centered thinking and planning—they have gone through the words and values, but the words and values haven't "gone through" them.

Person-centered thinking and planning isn't about the plan, the paper or applying the right technique. It's not about following the correct procedure or having one meeting and asking a person what she wants, writing it down, and following up on it quarterly or at an annual meeting. **In its most noble and virtuous meaning, person-centered planning is about relationships, caring for each other and helping everyone involved live a better life.**

Not Listening

There are a lot of things we can do to shoot ourselves in the foot in our efforts to engage in person-centered thinking and planning. We can leave important people out of the process, have a bad match between the person supported and the champion, be unaware of the most effective coaching techniques, over-manage the trivial and have non-productive meetings. As is now perhaps obvious, there are innumerable things that can go wrong—and some will. What is important is to self-correct as quickly as possible.

One error is of utmost concern—not listening to the person served or to those working to support her. Once again, the seminal thinkers in the person-centered design dialogue have words to share. In "Learning to Listen," John and Connie O'Brien stress the importance of listening and note that **"listening liberates energy; we, in fact, listen best when we encourage the person to find their voice."** How we listen is critical to understanding. They state the following:

> *People come to life when they make contact with someone who works actively and faithfully to understand what they want to say. When people communicate in unconventional ways, or when they have been rendered invisible by an environment that discounts the worth of their communication, the effects of listening can be profoundly energizing. Those who communicate without words, those who use words and symbols in unique ways, and those who communicate within the drama of their behavior call on their listeners' whole emotional, mental, and spiritual selves. They remind us that listening is much more than passing strings of words from mouth to ear. Listening is resonating in body, in imagination, and in spirit. Listening to people who live with the consequences of a lifetime of isolation and discrimination is often painful, frightening, and exciting.[31]*

More recently, positive psychology researchers have also been stressing the importance of active listening, not only for the purposes of clear communication, but also to recognize the positive emotions of a good conversation. Birgit Ohlin identifies the most common mistakes when listening:

1. Daydreaming or thinking of something else (thinking about or making up your list of groceries to be purchased) while another person is speaking
2. Thinking of what to say next
3. Judging what the other person is saying
4. Listening with a specific goal/outcome in mind.[32]

In seeking to emphasize the importance of listening, we encourage the reader to read *More Time to Think* by Nancy Kline (2015). Those people who may be working as champions with people with disabilities would find it particularly beneficial. For instance, she states that:

> *The quality of everything human beings do, everything—everything— depends on the quality of the thinking we do first. . . .*

> *Over the years, we and our colleagues confirmed that the most important factor in whether or not people can think for themselves is how they are being treated by the people with them while they are thinking.*

> **The way people behave with each other actually determines the quality of their thinking. Behaviour in the listener is more important than IQ, education, experience or background in the thinker.**[33]

Attention, with respect to listening, Kline continues, is like a chemical catalyst:

> *A catalyst in biochemistry is an amazing thing. It is a substance that increases the rate of a change without being consumed or changed itself. A catalyst also lowers the energy required for the change, allowing the change to proceed more quickly or at a lower temperature.*

> *This is what Attention does. It brings about change in a person's thinking by firing up connections and leaps and divings. And, like a catalyst, this Attention is constant. It is not changed by what the thinker does. And so it is a steady resource for them. They can count on this Attention to hold fast, to be intelligent, unconfused, compassionate, unconsumed and unchanged by where their thinking is going. . . .*

Attention of this quality recognizes that listening to reply is different from listening to ignite. Most people, including most professionals, listen to reply. Most people take in what they are hearing just long enough to come up with something to say in response. They listened to comment, to advise, to diagnose, to determine a clever intervention, to direct. They are within seconds out of step and out of date with the Thinker. The Thinker knows this and their thinking slows down. They can sense the gradual, and then accelerated, revving to speak that people do as they listen. Listening to ignite is a focus on where the Thinker will go next and on the wonder of that human mind in front of us.[34]

External Obstacles to Implementation

The following discussion of external obstacles is shared, not as an excuse for less-than-ideal outcomes, but rather to make all stakeholders aware of the difficulties we face today in carrying out genuine person-centered planning. Readers need to be aware and use this knowledge to organize individual and collective action to remove the obstacles from the service and support system.

National Staffing Crisis

As stated in Chapter 1, the field of intellectual/developmental disabilities has never experienced a staff shortage of the magnitude presently occurring. It is very hard as a provider to do your best in person-centered planning when you are preoccupied with survival. Health and safety issues become paramount in staff shortage environments, and those concerns do not tend to be fully disclosed lest regulatory bodies suddenly appear and impose sanctions or use such words as "immediate jeopardy" or "Let's hold admissions." Unfortunately, many state human service or Medicaid departments as well as legislatures seem to be ignoring the staffing crisis. They actually seek to impose additional standards at a time when funding is not sufficient to meet the current ones.

The staffing shortage extends to all staff levels: nurses, case coordinators or managers, QIDPs, even drivers, and especially direct support staff. So, while a plan may have been written with the best of intentions and agreed-upon steps of accomplishment, the targeted actions may not have occurred. For instance, the person being supported may have wanted to attend a planned sporting event and needed two staff to accompany her, but the staff weren't available, so the trip was cancelled. These cancellations don't occur because of neglect. **No staff member wants to break a promise to someone they care about. Clearly, insufficient staffing is by far the most serious obstacle to plan implementation.** While a provider can try to recruit volunteers to make these outings possible—in and of itself not an easy task— attempting to recruit staff that don't exist is obviously impossible.

Regulatory Requirements

Most experienced stakeholders in the disability field realize that federal and state regulations are primarily in place to stop bad things from happening. It should be noted, however, that good things don't suddenly appear—even when bad things are stopped. Regulations rarely serve the purpose of creating or enabling flexible, best or promising practices. The sheer magnitude of the ever-increasing requirements clearly bogs down authentic person-centered planning. Appropriate rules are indeed necessary, but so often, the authors of the rules do not understand the actual implications or ramifications of their actions. Numerous examples exist that could illustrate regulatory dysfunction, so in the context of this chapter on plan implementation, discussion will once again highlight the importance of separating needed documentation.

It is very hard as a provider to do your best in person-centered planning when **you are preoccupied with survival.**

A Separate Person-Centered Plan and Person-Centered Record

As mentioned previously but now stated succinctly, there should be two separate, but linked, person-centered documents: a person-centered plan and a person-centered record. Combining the two documents into one subordinates the person's real goals, needs and desires to legal and bureaucratic concerns. Obviously, different rules need to be written and adopted from a better design perspective. The current system of documentation and record keeping isn't supporting the purpose for which it was intended.

Think about a metaphoric person-centered planning chest of drawers with six drawers. The "My Plan to Flourish" or other, genuine person-centered plan is on top of the chest within easy sight and reach. The drawers of the chest are all useful to the planning process.

- The first drawer might be relevant assessments, inventories, preference tools, social history, and similar relevant information.
- The second drawer might be the person's health record, medication concerns and medical information.
- The third drawer might be the person's legal status, guardianship papers, and if applicable, rights and restrictions, etc.
- The fourth drawer might be a challenging behavior drawer, if needed, or any other safety or environmental concerns.
- The fifth drawer might contain records relevant to the person's history of receiving services and supports.
- The sixth drawer might be the junk drawer containing all the required information that isn't pertinent to the person but satisfies regulatory requirements.

So here's the question: If the purpose of person-centered planning is to help people enjoy a higher quality of life and live their best possible life, **why do they have to haul the entire weighty chest of drawers to a meeting about life plans? Why can't they just grab the plan that's sitting on the top of the chest of drawers?**

CHAPTER 10

The Organizational Inventory of Person-Centeredness

"Perfection is achieved, not when
there is nothing more to add, but when
there is nothing left to take away."
—Antoine de Saint-Exupery

A lot of territory has been covered thus far regarding person-centeredness that ranges from the importance of culture, planning, goal setting, positive psychology and well-being to an introduction to a new planning approach, "My Plan to Flourish."

The philosophy and practice of person-centered planning emanate most easily from a positive, values-driven organizational culture. Therefore, when organizations evaluate their practices of person-centered planning, it is also important to reflect on those organizational dynamics that clearly influence the success or failure of that intent.

The following inventory has been designed to examine the structure, organizational architecture and operational practices that influence person-centered outcomes most heavily.

Organizational Inventory
of Person-Centeredness©

1. The Board of Directors is knowledgeable and supportive of person-centered thinking and planning.

○ Rarely　○ Not Often　○ Occasionally　○ Often　○ Almost Always

2. The leadership staff of the organization are genuinely committed to the philosophy, principles and practices of person-centeredness.

○ Rarely　○ Not Often　○ Occasionally　○ Often　○ Almost Always

3. Persons served and supported as well as their family and friends are partners in the person-centered journey.

○ Rarely　○ Not Often　○ Occasionally　○ Often　○ Almost Always

4. Staff development efforts and training activities are fully immersed in person-centeredness.

○ Rarely　○ Not Often　○ Occasionally　○ Often　○ Almost Always

5. Ongoing quality improvement processes include monitoring person-centered practices.

○ Rarely　○ Not Often　○ Occasionally　○ Often　○ Almost Always

6. The employee evaluation system utilized by the organization includes a focus on person-centeredness.

○ Rarely   ○ Not Often   ○ Occasionally   ○ Often   ○ Almost Always

7. Working with a person supported to develop a meaningful life plan is of high importance to the organization.

○ Rarely   ○ Not Often   ○ Occasionally   ○ Often   ○ Almost Always

8. Direct support staff demonstrate a commitment to a person-centered, person-supporting career.

○ Rarely   ○ Not Often   ○ Occasionally   ○ Often   ○ Almost Always

9. Champions of person-centeredness are available to provide consultation and support throughout the organization.

○ Rarely   ○ Not Often   ○ Occasionally   ○ Often   ○ Almost Always

10. Visitors, guests, and regulatory bodies recognize that the organization has prioritized person-centeredness as a keystone value.

○ Rarely   ○ Not Often   ○ Occasionally   ○ Often   ○ Almost Always

The person-centered organizational inventory consists of ten measurement variables that reflect important elements, such as the governance level, employee commitment and the presence of champions. It's important to note the response status for each question as well as any trends or concerns across all ten of the questions.

Using the Organizational Inventory of Person-Centeredness®

The approach to completing the inventory is not prescriptive, given the different size and complexity of provider organizations. One approach is for the CEO and top management staff to complete the inventory individually and privately, and then compare the responses to each question across the entire team. Certain situations may foster greater openness if the responses included are done anonymously. There are obviously many other variations on the theme that could include having senior, non-administrative staff participate in the process.

Developing a Plan of Action

Whatever the method an organization chooses to complete the Organizational Inventory of Person-Centeredness®, it will quite likely identify areas needing improvement. Those evaluating the responses must come to agreement with respect to any conclusions drawn from survey responses for each of the ten questions. When in doubt, go with the lower rating. The goal is improvement, not self-satisfaction. Tabulating the responses across the dimensions of "rarely," "not often," "occasionally," "often," or "almost always" will offer a measurement and future comparison.

The goal is improvement, not self-satisfaction.

Of course, the reliability of the instrument depends on the honesty of those persons completing it. In addition, raters knowledgeable of the content areas are also essential. Finally, agency scoring is most helpful if it reflects more than one person's input.

After establishing that baseline, **the real work of getting better can begin.** The most common approach follows a typical project completion format, such as creating an organization-wide committee with a well-respected person as the chair. Committee members should agree on the landscape scan of the assessment results, and the subsequent priorities and concerns to be addressed. In addition, they must establish timelines and monitor progress.

We have been pleased with the feedback we have received from providers who have used this inventory. In Chapter 11, we present other lessons and suggestions that will further strengthen an organization and promote a positive, values-affirming culture.

Sustaining the Effort: Words of Encouragement

"He [she] who can't endure the bad will not live to see the good."

—Jewish Proverb

Lessons from Home Remodeling

We suspect that many readers have had the experience of those young couples who find themselves buying an old home that's affordable because it's in need of repair, redecorating or remodeling. Perhaps ancient wallpaper had to be scraped off, floors sanded and re-finished, and woodwork stripped and re-stained. You know the drill. You were excited at first and eagerly sought out paint swatches and watched the current home fixer-upper shows on TV.

The first room wasn't too bad, and it really looked good. But the second room became more of a challenge. You began to think that perhaps the woodwork could just be painted or repainted. The reality of what you had committed yourself to began to set in— and it wasn't that much fun anymore. The excitement vanished, and the home remodeling shows became burdensome reminders of what was to come.

Discouragement almost always arrives at the half-way point in the project, when the couple comes to understand how difficult the project really is and what it will take to sustain their efforts. Some couples stay with it and energize themselves by picturing the result. The goal is still motivating, and they continue on even though it's daunting. Other couples give up, decide to sell the home and find a new one that has already been sanded, stained and painted. Still other couples quit the project and their marriages, and go off on their separate ways.

> "You can't go back and change the beginning, **but you can start where you are and change the ending.**"
> —C.S. Lewis

C.S. Lewis offers some safe advice to those struggling in the middle: "You can't go back and change the beginning, but you can start where you are and change the ending."[35]

Organizational Grit

Let's look at the issue of realizing goals, doing hard work and sustaining effort through another lens, the lens of organizational grit. Grit is a construct that has been researched, and more widely shared as a result of Angela Duckworth's book, *Grit: The Power of Passion and Perseverance*, first published in 2016.

In a *Harvard Business Review* article (2018), Duckworth and Thomas Lee apply the concept of grit to health care. Clearly, their findings are also applicable to the human services sector, and specifically to supports and services for people with disabilities and the provider community. To accurately assess the hard work and discipline required for person-centered planning, readers are encouraged to read the book and the article.

In the article, Duckworth and Lee share some highlights of their experience in strengthening and developing gritty organizations. The Cleveland Clinic and Mayo Clinic serve as the exemplary providers. They note that the two key building blocks necessary for improving organizational performance are: 1) gritty individuals and 2) gritty teams.[36]

The key characteristics of gritty individuals are passion and perseverance. Not surprisingly, in the context of this book, **meaningfulness and purpose are the engines of grit.** Hiring people with grit is critical since they must be "unambiguously committed to the top level good—putting patients' needs above all else." (Mayo Clinic)[37]

The authors note that the essential element for growing gritty individuals and teams is "a demanding and supportive environment." As might be expected, gritty teams share the same characteristics as gritty individuals. They have a common sense of purpose and agreed-upon priorities, are committed to continuous improvement, work hard, and are resilient.[38]

Also important to the success of the grittiest teams is personal, in-the-room, face-to-face interactions and conversations. Think back to the support teams or circles of support and the crafting of person-centered plans where these kinds of connections and conversations are essential. The authors state that the goal should be championing the best teams, not the best individuals. This should also guide person-centered planning since a major responsibility of champions is to develop the best teams that can be mobilized to assist the person being supported.[39]

What is produced by gritty teams and individuals is a first class "putting patients first" culture that has a gritty leader at the helm. This leader is a role model who is supportive and demanding, but also a competent and strategic decision-maker.

What's the Point?

Those who work in human service organizations realize that permanent victories are rare in the work that we do. They also understand that the construction process of any important undertaking is much slower than the time in which it can be destroyed. We share an example of this phenomenon with total awareness that the goal of every high performing organization is to create systems that maintain the highest quality outcomes irrespective of the comings and goings of staff.

The setting could be a residential site or small day program. A senior leader, one that "gets it" unexpectedly leaves the organization because of his spouse's job change to another city. No one anticipated the resignation, and there is no obvious or qualified successor working at the site. So the organization's administrators hire a new person who out-shined other applicants in the interview process. However, after a short time, they discover that he lacks the same work ethic, knowledge and commitment as the former leader. Worse yet, the staff do not like him. You know what's coming next—a deterioration in the quality of supports and an environment that was once a source of pride is now a major problem.

So much of what we do in leadership is about people and relationships, and that's why we have often said, "Who we hire is the most important thing we do."

There's another important observation to keep in mind when working to sustain efforts and maintain quality supports—**"people leak and people stray."**[40] We all do. It's a function of our humanity. With that in mind, we have an obligation to attend to our staff promptly when we detect leaking and straying. "What does it look like?" you might ask. It's when we lose our focus, forget the mission of the organization, depart from our goal of putting the people we serve first, and become organization-centered rather than person-centered. What we must do is assist our staff so that they can fill themselves back up and find their way back to true north. On occasion, we must do the same for ourselves.

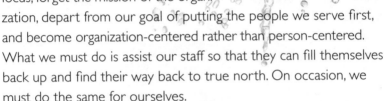

Not only are person-centered organizations difficult to sustain—defined by the ongoing improvement in people's lives with respect to well-being—so is the matter of genuine person-centered planning. "My Plan to Flourish" has been designed to be user friendly, easily grasped and communicated, and, most importantly, valued by the persons using it to improve their lives.

Crafting the actual plan is the easy part. The hard part is establishing and maintaining the relationships with those who have connected with the person and are supporting him. Person-centered planning is never done. Its success inevitably depends on people willing to work in person-centered ways.

The Importance of a Positive Outlook

Today, many researchers, authors, preachers and teachers are making us aware of the advantage of having a positive mindset in all areas of our lives—health, work performance, relationships, and, indeed, life satisfaction itself. And the evidence is compelling.

But being a positivist doesn't mean that we should avoid experiencing pain, listening to Mozart's "Requiem in D Minor," reading "Crossing the Bar" by Alfred Lord Tennyson, or denying the learning that comes from setbacks or failure. What it does mean is that we as optimists believe things can get better and that we can get better. Likewise, systems of support can be improved upon, advanced and strengthened.

Having a Benefit Mindset

Many readers are probably familiar with the work of Carol Dweck, with respect to mindsets—the aggregate of a person's attitude, beliefs and values that shape his behavior. Dweck's research led to the understanding that we choose our mindset and that such choices impact our learning, relationships, and even the success of our careers. In brief, a fixed mindset tends to shut us down, limiting our learning. A growth mindset, on the other hand, promotes learning and goal accomplishment.[41]

Ash Buchanan, a positive psychologist and consultant, proposes yet a third construct, the *benefit mindset.* This perspective builds on the growth mindset but moves the construct beyond how we seek to do better and improve our personal performance to focusing on why we do what we do. The emphasis is on collective well-being, not just personal well-being.

Proponents are fond of saying "from being the best to being the best for others."[42] It is not surprising that so many champions and staff working to support people with disabilities exhibit a benefit mindset and a life of service.

Look for People with a Calling

Martin Seligman had grown quite dissatisfied with the emphasis
on the past and present in current psychology. So he recruited three
colleagues, Peter Railton, Roy F. Baumeister and Chandra Sripada,
to join him in creating a new starting point for a more enlightened
approach. One of their conclusions was that "discovering what
the person expects, intends and desires in the future is usually a better
starting point than asking about past behavior." Homo sapiens as
"thinking man" was no longer an adequate description of our species.

In the resulting work, Homo Prospectus (2016), the researchers

> ...use the term prospection as a label for the mental process of
> projecting and evaluating future possibilities and then using these
> projections for the guidance of thought and action (Buckner &
> Carroll, 2007; Gilbert & Wilson, 2007). Like an old-time prospector
> searching for gold, the mind's processes of prospection map out
> not just the physical landscape lying ahead, but an array of possible
> paths through that landscape. Like an old-time prospector, too,
> the mind must select among these paths in the face of uncertainty
> and partial information. So an estimation must be made of the
> promise of the different paths relative to sought-after goals, given
> the likely risks and costs.[43]

The notion of prospection is that human beings are unique since they
alone are continuously thinking about and looking into the future.
As a result, we engage in mental representations of the future as well
as evaluate possible outcomes of prospection, including daydreaming,
planning, attempting to anticipate the future, imagining personal future
scenarios and even predicting future emotional states, identified as
affective forecasting.

While Seligman's purpose in exploring a different approach was not to
discern the character of prospective employees, his research—though
a bit cerebral—got us thinking in a more pragmatic fashion. As leaders

in organizations serving and supporting people with disabilities, what are we looking for in job applicants? Staying with the metaphor, when prospecting with a metal detector, one can set the controls for a finer discrimination with a phase shift that will allow one to discern, for example, steel or iron from silver or gold. And when the search begins, treasure hunters are told to stay "low and slow" with their search.

So here's the question: **"As leaders, what are we prospecting for?"** Some people are bent toward the negative, others toward the positive. That's a big question that we ask readers to consider. For purposes of this particular application, the specific question is, "What kind of employees will be the most successful in person-centered planning and the accompanying person-centered work environments?"

The good news is that there are still people who want to help others, but we might have to search for them. Look for people who have a calling, whether secular or religious, those who want to be part of something greater than themselves. We always have a need for positive influencers. And while you are at it, as Andy Stanley has suggested, hire doers over thinkers. You can always teach a doer how to think better, but it's a lot harder to get a thinker moving.

In addition, when you employ people powered by purpose, they may sometimes become quickly discouraged by obstacles, namely paperwork. It is important that we spend enough time with them so that they understand that paperwork is a small price to pay for helping someone have a better life. And by all means, work to reduce the paperwork.

A Quick Look at Community Acceptance

> "We could love those neighbors wondrous
> if, instead of next door,
> they lived several blocks from us."
> —Ogden Nash

Trinity Services, like many other providers across the country, serves people living with their families and also those living in homes and apartments. One of our goals—and one of *their* goals—is for the people we support to be an integral part of the community.

Every year we do a fun research project on Halloween and count the number of youngsters who come to the doors of the homes where people are living with 24-hour supports in the community. The Halloween experience at Trinity is very positive, not only for the people we support, but for the neighborhood. The numbers are high and appropriate to the community. All it takes is some candy. Of course, we realize that in some communities the "trick-or-treating practices" are being frowned upon and also that some neighborhoods have a higher percentage of children than others.

Feel free to try this simple research project in your community.

Overcoming Labels

There's no doubt that the early years of the person-centered movement rightfully emphasized the importance of social justice and
the need for full inclusion for all persons, disabled or not. As progress
unfolded, new terms and role descriptions came into being in the
disability world. For example, the term "self-advocate" was borrowed
from the broader civil rights movement and soon individuals with
disabilities identified themselves as self-advocates. Other folks joined
in and helped develop the role description of self-advocate. What
the term meant was that people with disabilities wanted to speak for
themselves, to have control over their lives. No doubt some self-
advocates enjoyed the edginess of the descriptor and sometimes the
attendant attention.

However, as so often happens, the term became shorthand for
"persons with intellectual disabilities," and as could have been predicted,
"self-advocates" is how people with disabilities are often identified
today. Check out national and state websites, let alone publications,
and notice how frequently you see such language as, "If you're a
self-advocate, register here," "Ask for the self-advocate discount," or
"Add a self-advocate to your committee."

**The reality is that the voice of people with disabilities is being heard
much more today.** A growing number of people, especially young
people graduating from high school, do not like the term or its infer-
ence. Cameron, a young man with an intellectual disability, recently
told us that he "hated the name 'self-advocate.'" To him, it was the same
thing as being labeled—and this is his word—"retarded." While the
self-determining battles aren't over, many people that we serve are
interested in things beyond themselves, beyond how they are treated
or what they're called. More and more individuals receiving supports
are interested in the plastic floating in oceans, the violence in inner
cities and resolving racial tensions. After our conversation, Cameron
said he wanted to be a community activist. He wanted to be just like
everybody else.

Before leaving the topic of language and identity, we would like to suggest that another term be laid to rest, the term "consumer." This word illustrates another case in which a specific social role became a thing unto itself. "If she ain't a self-advocate, she's a consumer," a frustrated mother of a 20-year-old daughter with cerebral palsy stated recently. "Why can't she just be a person?"

It's likely that everyone reading this book is okay with their understanding that on many occasions they are a consumer, but it is not their identity. Worse yet, among many people and their families, it suggests that a person with a disability can never be a producer, only a user, a consumer.

Positive Developments and Future Possibilities

As stated earlier, systems of support can be both bad and better. We are grateful for the progress that has occurred in the lives of all people, including those with disabilities. The following pages reflect positive developments, wide-ranging ideas, and some suggestions that will continue to make the system better in the future. We share them as themes and words of encouragement as we bring this book to a close.

We have already discussed the need for additional direct support staff and acknowledged that the problem may continue for some time given the current level of funding. It is quite likely that there will simply not be enough direct support staff to go around in the future—especially if one notes the growing aging population and their support needs. Therefore, human service providers need to focus on creative solutions to this dilemma. We offer three ideas below—the use of assistive technology, support coaches and the creative use of social technology.

> "If she ain't a self-advocate, she's a consumer,"... **"Why can't she just be a person?"**

Use of Assistive Technology

We've known that assistive technology should play an important part in the lives of people with disabilities for a long time. Now, more than ever, technology "levels the playing field" for people with disabilities— it promotes independence, breaks down barriers and fosters inclusion.

The generally accepted definition of assistive technology is "any product, piece of equipment, or program—whether acquired commercially off the shelf, modified, or customized—that is used to increase, maintain, or improve the functional capabilities of a person with a disability." The scope of assistive technology is broad and solutions range from "high tech" (i.e., tablets, environmental controls and robotics, among other things) to "low tech" (i.e., adaptive eating utensils, bath lifts, reachers, and similar helps).

Remote supports are one form of technology that has been hotly debated in recent years. Essentially, it can be defined as the use of equipment to oversee, monitor and supervise someone from a remote location. There are a number of credible, third-party vendors who provide this service, but some organizations and families have chosen to develop their own systems. The use of sensors, cameras and other equipment in residential settings is not a new idea, but what is remarkable is the slow pace at which it is being adopted across the United States or certainly, for that matter, the low extent to which it is being piloted. This is especially noteworthy given the staffing shortages occurring across the country.

Remote support equipment encompasses a variety of devices. It can include, but is not limited to:

- Audio listening devices
- Cameras and video equipment
- Mobile, on-person equipment (e.g., body sensors, GPS tracking)
- Sensors not on the person (e.g., motion sensors, door and window alarms).

In general, it is used to achieve one or more of the following objectives:

- Increase independence
- Address a complex medical condition or other extreme circumstance
- Reduce or minimize critical incidents
- Improve the quality of supports.

In order for remote supports to be implemented, it must be the most appropriate means (and the person's preferred method) to address assessed needs and goals. There should be a thoughtful planning process that occurs before implementation. Considerations should include:

- Where will the technology be implemented?
- What is the purpose of using the technology?
- What type of equipment will meet the person's needs and goals?
- How will the person request in-person supports when they are needed?
- Who will respond to in-person support requests?
- What are the contingency plans for emergency situations (i.e., staff shortage, inclement weather, internet/power outages, and the like)?
- What payment or funding options are available?

The image of Homer Simpson sitting behind a large monitoring screen asleep doesn't help allay the fears of people who insist on 24-hour-awake staff to support their loved ones. However, a targeted campaign to educate people about the possibilities brought about by the use of remote supports would be helpful. This, when paired with meaningful discussion and thoughtful planning, can increase buy-in from families, service providers and state officials.

It is indeed likely that in the future there will simply not be enough direct support staff to go around—especially if one notes the growing aging population and their support needs. The implementation of remote support technology is one method for addressing this staffing shortage, but it is not a magic solution that will work for all people in all situations.

Though remote supports have gotten a lot of attention, it is important to remember that this is only one type of technology that can help increase and maintain independence for people. Even in cases where remote supports are identified as the best option for a person, other types of technology will likely be needed to offer comprehensive supports. For this reason, we encourage providers to reach out to local and national resources to explore technology options for the people they support.

Voice Assistant Technology

Amazon's Alexa, Apple's Siri, Microsoft's Cortana, and Google Assistant are changing the world of disabilities by giving people new daily living options through voice power.

It is now easy to check the weather, sports scores and even maintain a daily calendar all through voice interaction with these voice-activated virtual assistants. People who are visually impaired can check the time, schedule a ride, play audio books and get a world of answers from "browsing" the web.

People who are physically challenged can, by simply asking, control the thermostat, raise and lower blinds, lock a door or storage cabinet, play music, turn lights off and on, and much more through the growing array of voice assistant skills. Safety can be enhanced by installing detectors that tell residents what is being detected: smoke, natural gas, carbon monoxide, even a water leak. Most smart home devices include integration with at least one type of voice technology. Almost one third of homes use smart devices now, moving toward a predicted one half of homes by 2022. A computer is not even required—all smartphones now include voice technology.

Some of the ways those who have intellectual or developmental disabilities use voice assistants include:

- Asking Siri to type and send emails or texts
- Requesting a ride through an Uber or Lyft app
- Ordering groceries to be delivered
- Navigating while riding, biking or walking
- "Reading" ebooks.

The ability to easily set reminders can be like having a virtual coach. "Joel, it's time to call for your ride to Karen's party." Reminders can tell someone when to get ready for work, take medication, or go outside for a walk. It's just as easy to ask a voice assistant to set a timer. "Alexa, remind me in twelve minutes that the pasta is ready." Since many voice devices can access (and create) playlists, it's possible to ask a device to play "On the Road Again" when it's time to leave for work, "Happy" when it's time to exercise, or "Claire de Lune" when it's time to get ready for bed.

Watches are now speaking to us as well. An Apple Watch can report the weather or record a voice memo. The latest Fitbit watches announce how close a person is to their daily step goal.

Access to this relatively inexpensive and easy-to-use technology is bringing greater independence to many people with disabilities.

Support Coaches: Responding to the Staffing Crisis Impacting Persons with Developmental Disabilities

Today, in almost every community, there is a shortage of service and support employees. The immediate consequence of having too few employees is both scary and devastating. For example, it is not unusual for a group home to have only one person on duty when the staffing pattern might call for two staff, or even three. Direct support staff are burning out from working too many shifts while having too little sleep. Bad things start to happen when staff are sleep deprived and work excessively long in stressful environments.

All of this creates environments where staff turnover is at an all-time high, resulting in extraordinary training costs. More concerning, however, is the negative impact on the people served who now lack much needed continuity. Think how you would feel in a classroom where you had a new teacher every day.

There is an action that can be taken within the developmental disabilities service system to help combat the current staffing crisis—the employment of support coaches. While it is common practice to use job coaches in the employment arena, we are not aware of any organized effort to create the position of support coach or a comprehensive model incorporating their use.

The support coach model has been successful with individuals diagnosed with attention deficit/hyperactivity disorder (ADHD). ADHD coaching essentially consists of helping a person address, cope with, or overcome their primary impairments—distraction, impulsivity, time management, problem-solving ability, goal setting, etc.[44]

ADHD coaches work collaboratively with their clients around specific problem areas as well as personal goals. Similarly, support coaches hired by a person with a disability or their family can assist a person across the many dimensions of their life—education, work, interpersonal relationships and residential living, among others. There are, however, role boundaries: coaches do not serve as therapists or personal care assistants, although they might help coordinate these staff.

Training for support coaches would follow the contributions of positive psychology and include important skills, such as anger management, mindfulness, emotional regulation, and other pertinent areas.

Support coaches do not have to be present on a 24-hour basis. They can be available by phone, text or appointment. Coaching varies from minimal to intensive, depending on the person or situation.

Coaching can take place in group settings as well as individual sessions. Support coaches could work under the umbrella of a provider organization; however, the coach-client relationship, including hiring, scope of services, and termination would be between the coach and person supported.

The result is that the persons coached feel more in charge of their lives, experience greater self-esteem and more self-reliance.[45]

Here is the value-added dimension. **There are many people who have a developmental disability who could, with appropriate training and guidance, work as support coaches themselves,** thus adding to the available workforce.

There is also a major systems implication. As adults, people with developmental and intellectual disabilities are typically served or supported in a wide variety of employment options, structured day programs, and an array of residential alternatives from supported homes to apartment living, group homes, adult foster care or small facilities. Many persons with developmental disabilities are over-served in a 24-hour-a-day, supervised environment. With careful assessment and preparation, many could move to other environments and be successful with the addition of a support coach, making it possible for more persons on waiting lists to be served in the resulting vacancies.

Social Technology and What Lies Ahead

Just as assistive technology and the employment of support coaches represent areas of much greater possibility for persons with intellectual disabilities— especially in self-determination and increased independence—so does the potential of social technology and its applications. Generally speaking, when we hear the term social technology, we think of digital networks, such as Facebook, Instagram, Twitter, Snapchat, and others. There is no doubt that such conversation platforms are rapidly impacting all areas of our lives: business, industry, human services and our personal relationships.

> We are enthused with respect to **the future applications of social technology for people with disabilities.**

Recently, professors at the University of Lithuania reviewed the literature in a paper entitled "Defining Social Technologies." They observed that social technology

> ...could be used for various purposes such as decision making, knowledge sharing, etc.

> Social technologies can be defined as any technologies used for goals of social interaction or with any social basis, including social hardware (traditional communication media), social software (computer mediated media), and social media (social networking tools) (Alberghini, et al, 2010). Chui et al (2012) defines social technologies 'as digital technologies used by people to interact socially and together to create, enhance and exchange content.'[46]

The authors describe social technologies from three dimensions:

- Richness: 'the ability to convey verbal and nonverbal cues, and facilitate shared meaning in a timely manner';
- Interactivity: 'the extent to which rapid feedback is allowed';
- Social presence: 'the degree to which virtual team members feel close to one another.'[47]

They conclude that research indicates that social technology is a powerful digital means of connecting people socially in ways that offer "pleasure and intellectual stimulation" as they share their opinions and learn from others. The technology is advancing rapidly and being used by "80 percent of the world's online population with impressive results in professional and business activities." That said, "65 percent of the world population—4.6 billion people—still lacks internet access." Clearly, as social technologies become more widely available and are applied in many more contexts, development will increase exponentially.[48]

Before continuing, please know in the context of the above paragraph that we are also well aware of the fact that many people with disabilities in this country do not have access to computers and mobile devices. It is another one of those areas in which we have to work together to create the necessary change that is required.

Nevertheless, we are enthused with respect to the future applications of social technology for people with disabilities. Again, we are well aware of the fact that people vary in their ability to master such devices as iPads and smartphones, but we also believe the technology advances will unfold to include more and more people.

It is clear that future applications will improve safety, decrease social isolation, provide greater assistance in problem solving, create greater opportunities for collaboration, and yes, even strengthen an individual's ability to achieve their goals through group support.

Social Technology Use in Goals Support Groups

As we write, Trinity Services is developing a prototype Goals Support Group using social technology for the people it supports. The group's members participate in an innovative Community Day Services program. Each member has some ability to read and write, and each uses a smartphone. Group members use a mobile app to help them encourage each other's progress as well as help other members reach their own goals.

Staff are encouraged by the group members' enthusiasm for the project. Their goals range from wanting to be on time for work to finding a boyfriend/girlfriend. They're excited about using the considerable technology they carry every day to help them achieve something truly important to them.

During the first few group sessions, the members learned about the elements of well-being with discussions about emotions, engagement, relationships, meaning, accomplishment, and health. These sessions led to conversations about goals—how just making progress on one step can add to well-being.

The Trinity Services Goals Support Group gets together in person mainly to have a context for accomplishing goals. The very purpose of the group is to achieve goals and help other members meet their goals. But they realized that each member could go much further if they were also able to find others who share their goal, others who have similar strengths, others who have already accomplished their goal and who have similar challenges. That's where social technology comes in.

At the same time, we do not underestimate the importance of real face-to-face personal contact, though we are avid supporters of social technology and all of its contributions.

Social Technology with Gamification

The most basic description of gamification is simply to make any task more like a game, to give a work task one or more elements of a recreational pastime. Yu-Kai Chou, in *Actionable Gamification* defines gamification as "…the craft of deriving fun and engaging elements found typically in games and thoughtfully applying them to real-world or productive activities."[49] A simple example is "playing" beat-the-clock while trying to finish a boring task (like cleaning a room) before a timer goes off. Amazingly, distracting yourself from the task by competing with the timer, determining to "beat" it to the punch (ring) adds just enough anticipation tension to motivate you to do more, faster. In other words, to up your game.

Back in 1984, Charles Coonradt talked about bringing the "Motivation of Recreation" to the workplace in his book, *The Game of Work*. According to Coonradt, the five principles of the Motivation of Recreation are:

- Clearly defined goals
- Better scorekeeping and scorecards
- More frequent feedback
- A higher degree of personal choice of methods
- Consistent coaching.[50]

As Coonradt was writing, video game software designers were hard at work designing games that made use of the ever-expanding capabilities of the digital world and, eventually, the internet. Video games are like classic recreational activities on steroids. One of the reasons some video games became popular almost to the point of addiction for some people is that game software designers were fascinated with the challenge of learning what kept gamers playing longer as well as what made them return to play more frequently. Every game iteration and program update was designed to deliver more of the anticipation and motivation hormone, dopamine, to users' brains as they played. In addition, many of the most popular games have a social aspect where players create and join teams, and together take on and complete compelling quests. Players encourage each other, adding a deeper layer of feeling—belonging to a trusted group on an important mission.

Jane McGonigal addresses the positive role that this technology offers in *SuperBetter*, the game she invented for herself to overcome a serious brain injury, and the title of her book that has taught hundreds of thousands of people to "live gamefully" and achieve epic personal wins. She states: "You are stronger than you know. You are surrounded by potential allies. You are the hero of your own story."[51]

The benefits of social technology for people with disabilities who use it to help them meet their goals is, at minimum, twofold: the motivation potential of an app (with reminders, anticipated rewards for completion, and game-like design) and the encouragement of kindred spirits who are on the same quest, cheering each other on.

A Few Words About Employee Motivation and Optimism

Employee Motivation

"The more removed we are from someone, the more likely we are to blame them."[52] That interesting quote comes from *Primed to Perform* by Neel Doshi and Lindsay McGregor. It's an insight nestled in a book that offers clear direction for getting better in the future through examining employee motivation and high performing cultures, reminding us of the importance of sustained effort and accomplishment in the face of implementation failure.

...we must focus renewed energy in creating positive work cultures where **both employees and those supported thrive and flourish.**

The authors share critical information with respect to how motives impact performance. Three are directly tied to the actual work performed—play, purpose and potential—and three others to indirect motives—emotional pressure, economic pressure and inertia, which are further removed from the work itself and "frequently harm performance."[53]

The key point is to realize that a high performing, person-centered organization will have a culture where its employees are primarily motivated through play—"engaging in an activity simply because they enjoy doing it—curiosity and experimentation are at the heart of play."[54] Purpose, on the other hand, occurs as a motivator when employees value the outcome of the activity—which is different from the activity itself. This takes place when the employees' values and beliefs are in line with the impact or outcomes of the work being performed. Finally, potential motivates when employees do the work because of what it can lead to, for example, the achievement of their personal goals.

Here's the take home message:
"A culture that inspires people to do their jobs for play, purpose, and potential creates the highest and most sustainable performance."[55]

Being a provider for persons with intellectual and developmental disabilities is not getting easier. Nevertheless, we must focus renewed energy in creating positive work cultures where both employees and those supported thrive and flourish.

The Importance of Optimism

We began this book with the observation that we undertook the task of rethinking person-centered planning from the perspective of being possibilists. That is, we recognize the shortcomings of implementation and the status of present human service "systems," but we are, nevertheless, firm believers that doing better is possible and achievable. To that end, we conclude with some thoughts on optimism.

We believe that those individuals working to support people with disabilities must do it with a positive and optimistic mindset. This is especially important for leadership staff and those working as champions. Our thoughts are not just passive events that occur inside our heads. They impact and influence our expectations and actions, and ultimately what transpires.

With that in mind, we can't imagine a person or family wanting to be supported by a habitually pessimistic person—who believes that failure is inevitable. These are the people who believe that bad things will last longer than they do, and as a result give up more quickly and get depressed more often.[56]

We are also fully aware that not everyone is an optimist or wants to be an optimist. In addition, we know that organizations benefit from including employees who are pessimistically inclined. They are the people who serve as variance sensors, caution our enthusiasm, worry about cash flow and balance sheets, and alert us to danger. These staff should not be confused, however, with the hard-core pessimists, who drain energy and actually undermine the spirit of an organization.

Martin Seligman argues in *Learned Optimism* that "an organization filled with optimistic individuals—or studded with optimistic individuals in the crucial niches—has an edge…. Optimistic individuals are known to produce more, particularly under pressure, than do pessimists."[57]

We believe this insight pertains to meaningful person-centered planning as well. It is our experience that plans are more likely to be fully implemented in positive, optimistic organizations.

It is also our experience that organizations headed by a CEO, who has a pessimistic explanatory style, do not do well with any person-centered model. This is also the case when pessimistic senior staff dominate in an organization. The system overwhelms them, the people of the state capitols ruin their day, and their perceived lack of staff or resources prevents their success. For them, the water is indeed continuously circling the drain.

But be of good cheer. We can choose the way we think, and that can change our lives and the lives of others as well.

"An organization filled with optimistic individuals... **has an edge...**"

CHAPTER 12

After Words: How to Get Better

"Choose better.

More honest, more caring, more generous.

It's all a choice, isn't it?

We can choose to dream better,
connect better and contribute better.

Sometimes, in the rush for more,
we get confused about what better means,
and how attainable it is."

—Seth Godin

How to get better

One thing at a time

Most important thing first

Start now!

Thanks to Caroline Webb,
How To Have A Good Day

ANewPlan.org

First, we would like to thank the Executive Leadership team of Trinity Services for their pioneer work in collaborating to create the "My Plan to Flourish" and also for their feedback in putting this book together. A special thanks to Sally Ritchey, Mike Mecozzi, Steph Behlke-Leigh, Christina Chavez and Tina Fogarty for their thoughtful comments and suggestions, together with Lisa Dillon, Sherry Ladislas, Ray Carmody, Michele Gossen, Jennifer Hodges, Sharon Parker Love, Dr. Ragani Patwari, Trina Sieling, Bob Taylor, Andy Long, Anita Goulding, Mike Lowry and Amy Roberts.

We would also like to thank Bob Sandidge and Anne Ward for their many contributions to this project, including content development, idea clarification and design.

Other Trinity staff we would like to recognize for their efforts are Charlie Egner, Connie Melvin, Rich Harrington, Jen Klouse, Alexis Haase, Susann Faulk, Michelle Mackler, Laura Neuhardt and Susan Conlon. As always, the encouragement of Jim and Elaine Nelson is valued and appreciated. Thane is most grateful to Kelsie Dykstra and Jarrod Dykstra for their unfailing love and support.

Special thanks go to Mary Rundell-Holmes for her great work and tireless efforts on the part of High Tide Press, and to John Sotirakis for his creativity in cover work and design. We are also grateful for the support efforts of Tara Garner and Beth Purdom.

We have very much appreciated the thinkers and leaders in the positive psychology movement, especially Martin Seligman. We are further indebted to our many friends and colleagues who reacted to our thoughts and ideas during the course of this endeavor.

Thank you.

1. The term was coined by Friedrich Ratzel (1844–1904), a German geographer and ethnographer.

2. Carol S. Dweck, *Mindset: The New Psychology of Success* (New York: Ballantine Books, 2008), pp. 6–11.

3. Hans Rosling, Ola Rosling, and Anna Rosling Ronnlund, *Factfulness: Ten Reasons We're Wrong About the World—and Why Things Are Better Than You Think* (New York: Flatiron Books, 2018), pp. 70–71.

4. McDonald's, "Archways to Opportunity," 2019, www.archwaystoopportunity.com.

5. Martin E.P. Seligman, *The Hope Circuit: A Psychologist's Journey from Helplessness to Optimism* (New York: Hachette Book Group, 2018), p. 5.

6. Brian Kim, "Why You Should Write Down Your Goals," *The Definitive Guide to Self-Improvement* (blog), 2016, http://briankim.net/articles/write-goals.

7. Kamran Akbarzadeh, "Seven Reasons Why We Avoid Planning Ahead and What to Do About Them," *Dream Achievers Academy* (blog), n.d., https://www.dreamachieversacademy.com/seven-reasons-why-we-avoid-planning-ahead.

8. Gunnar Dybwad, *Challenges in Mental Retardation* (New York: Columbia University Press, 1964), p. 208.

9. Bengt Nirje, "The Normalization Principle and Its Human Management Implications," in *Changing Patterns in Residential Services for the Mentally Retarded*, ed. Wolf P. Wolfensberger and Robert B. Kruegel (Washington, D.C.: President's Committee on Mental Retardation, 1969), p. 181.

10. For the full text of the handbook, see Wolf P. Wolfensberger and Linda Glenn, *Program Analysis of Service Systems (PASS 3): A Method for the Quantitative Evaluation of Human Services* (Toronto, Ontario, National Institute on Mental Retardation, 1975), https://digitalcommons.unmc.edu/wolf_books/2.

11. Susan Thomas and Wolf Wolfensberger, "An Overview of Social Role Valorization," in *A Quarter Century of Normalization and Social Role Valorization: Evolution and Impact*, ed. Robert J. Flynn and Raymond A. Lemay (Ottawa, Canada: University of Ottawa Press, 1999), pp. 135–139, 149–152.

12. John O'Brien, "A Guide to Personal Futures Planning," in *A Little Book About Person-Centered Planning*, ed. John O'Brien and Connie Lyle O'Brien (Lithonia, GA: Responsive Systems Associates, 1998), pp. 134–136.

13. John Swinton, "From Inclusion to Belonging: A Practical Theology of Community, Disability and Humanness," *Journal of Religion, Disability & Health* 16, no. 2 (April 2012): 172–190.

14. Martin E.P. Seligman, *Flourish: A Visionary New Understanding of Happiness and Well-Being* (New York: Free Press, 2011), p. 20.

15. Seligman, *Flourish*, pp. 14–15.

16. Seligman, *Flourish*, pp. 16–20.

17. Seligman, *Flourish*, p. 17.

18. Julie Butler and Margaret L. Kern, "The PERMA-Profiler: A Brief Multidimensional Measure of Flourishing," *International Journal of Wellbeing* 6, no. 3 (2016): 1–48.

19. The Council on Quality and Leadership, "Personal Outcome Measures," https://www.c-q-l.org/the-cql-difference/personal-outcome-measures.

20. Beth Mount, "More Than a Meeting: Benefits and Limitations of Personal Futures Planning," in *A Little Book About Person Centered Planning*, ed. John O'Brien and Connie Lyle O'Brien (Toronto, Ontario: Inclusion Press, 2007), p. 55.

21. Mary Mercer, *Person-Centered Planning: Helping People with Disabilities Achieve Personal Outcomes* (Homewood, IL: High Tide Press, 2003), p. 30.

22. Helen Sanderson and Jaimee Lewis, *A Practical Guide to Delivering Personalization: Person-Centred Practice in Health and Social Care* (London, England: Jessica Kingsley Pub., 2012), p. 25.

23. Shawn Achor, *Big Potential: How Transforming the Pursuit of Success Raises Our Achievement, Happiness, and Well-Being* (New York: Currency, 2018), p. 134.
24. Achor, *Big Potential,* p. 74.
25. Art Dykstra, *Outcome Management: Achieving Outcomes for People with Disabilities* (Homewood, IL: High Tide Press, 1995), p. 92.
26. Dykstra, *Outcome Management*, p. 93.
27. Seth Godin, "A Commitment to Possibility," *Seth's Blog*, December 24, 2018, https://seths.blog/2018/12/a-commitment-to-possibility.
28. Caroline Webb, *How to Have a Good Day: Harness the Power of Behavioral Science to Transform Your Working Life* (New York: Crown Publishing Group, 2016), p. 49.
29. Martha Lasley et al, *Coaching for Transformation: Pathways to Ignite Personal & Social Change*, 2nd ed. (Troy, PA: Discover Press, 2015), pp. 296–298.
30. Dykstra, *Outcome Management*, pp. 100–101.
31. John O'Brien and Connie Lyle O'Brien, "Learning to Listen," in *A Little Book About Person Centered Planning,* ed. John O'Brien and Connie Lyle O'Brien (Toronto, Ontario: Inclusion Press, 2007), p. 15.
32. Birgit Ohlin, "Active Listening: The Art of Empathetic Conversation," *PositivePsychology.com* (blog), July 21, 2016, https://positivepsychology.com/active-listening.
33. Nancy Kline, *More Time to Think: The Power of Independent Thinking* (London, England: Octopus Publishing Group, 2015), p. 15.
34. Kline, *More Time to Think*, pp. 35–36.
35. Widely attributed to C.S. Lewis though it has yet to be located in any of his published works.
36. Thomas H. Lee and Angela L. Duckworth, "Organizational Grit," *Harvard Business Review* 96, no. 5 (September-October 2018): 98–105.
37. Lee and Duckworth, "Organizational Grit," pp. 98–105.
38. Lee and Duckworth, "Organizational Grit," pp. 98–105.
39. Lee and Duckworth, "Organizational Grit," pp. 98–105.
40. Dykstra, *Outcome Management*, pp. 14–16.

41. Carol S. Dweck, *Mindset: The New Psychology of Success* (New York: Ballantine Books, 2008), p. 6–7.
42. Ash Buchanan and Margaret L. Kern, "The Benefit Mindset: The Psychology of Contribution and Everyday Leadership," *International Journal of Wellbeing* 7, no. 1: 2–4.
43. Martin E.P. Seligman et al, *Homo Prospectus* (New York: Oxford University Press, 2016), p. 6.
44. "Coaching," *Children and Adults with Attention-Deficit/Hyperactivity Disorder (CHADD)*, 2019, https://chadd.org/about-adhd/coaching.
45. "Coaching," https://chadd.org/about-adhd/coaching.
46. Aelita Skarzauskiene, Ruta Tamosiunaite and Inga Zaleniene, "Defining Social Technologies." Paper presented at the 4th International Conference on Information Systems Management and Evaluation, Ho Chi Ming City, Vietnam, January 2013, p. 240.
47. Skarzauskiene, Tamosiunaite and Zaleniene, "Defining Social Technologies," p. 240.
48. Skarzauskiene, Tamosiunaite and Zaleniene, "Defining Social Technologies," p. 244.
49. Yu-Kai Chou, *Actionable Gamification: Beyond Points, Badges and Leaderboards* (Milpitas, CA: Octalysis Media, 2017), p. 8.
50. Charles A. Coonradt, *The Game of Work: How to Enjoy Work As Much As Play* (Layton, UT: Gibbs Smith, 2012), p. 2.
51. Jane McGonigal, *SuperBetter: The Power of Living Gamefully* (New York: Penguin Books, 2016), p. 1.
52. Neel Doshi and Lindsay McGregor, *Primed to Perform: How to Build the Highest Performing Culture Through the Science of Total Motivation* (New York: Harper Business, 2015), p. 74.
53. Doshi and McGregor, *Primed to Perform*, p. 7.
54. Doshi and McGregor, *Primed to Perform*, p. 7.
55. Doshi and McGregor, *Primed to Perform*, p. 9.
56. Martin E.P. Seligman, *Learned Optimism: How to Change Your Mind and Your Life* (New York: Vintage Books, 2006), pp. 4–5.
57. Seligman, *Learned Optimism*, p. 256.

About the Authors

Art Dykstra, CEO of the Trinity Foundation and the Cherry Hill Consulting Group, is a well-known author and speaker whose major interest is leadership development, organizational culture and working to support persons with disabilities.

He is the author of numerous publications, including *Outcome Management* and *Creating a Positive Organizational Culture,* and with Tim Williams co-authored *Gossip! You Won't Believe This.*

Art has served on state and national boards of directors and chaired many of them. He has been a university faculty member, organizational consultant and program advisor. He is a fellow of the American Association on Intellectual Disabilities.

Art and his wife, Anita, live in the Chicago suburbs. In his spare time he enjoys fishing, gardening and bike riding.

Art and Thane Dykstra

Thane Dykstra, Ph.D. currently serves as the President and CEO of Trinity Services, a non-profit, non-sectarian organization that serves individuals with cognitive impairments and/or mental illness through-out the State of Illinois in a wide array of programs. Trinity's home office is in New Lenox, Illinois.

Thane is a past president of the Illinois Association of Behavior Analysis, and serves on many boards of directors and advisory groups. He has authored numerous professional publications, including being the lead author and developer of the Community Crisis Risk Management Assessment. He is a frequent conference speaker. He has a special fondness for working with persons with mental illness and intellectual disabilities who exhibit challenging behavior.

Thane lives in Chicago's south suburbs with his wife Kim, two cats and one dog. His special pet, a ferret named Bandit, will always be remembered. Thane enjoys camping, hiking, fishing and disc golf.

Trinity Services, Inc. was founded in 1950 by families of children with intellectual disabilities, who came together to seek services that were not offered in schools at the time. From the beginning, the non-profit, non-sectarian organization sought to provide the highest quality services and supports so that people could flourish and live full and abundant lives.

Located in New Lenox, Illinois, Trinity serves over 4,000 individuals throughout Illinois in more than 31 communities. With a staff of over 1,100 employees, Trinity operates a wide range of services and programs—including a large residential program that provides many options, a school, community day services that offer a variety of innovative approaches, community employment opportunities, respite services, an assistive "tech lab," and many other vital support services.

Trinity Services also supports people with mental illness in residential and day support services, and provides employment preparation and placement. Other programs include a counseling center and out-patient treatment options. In addition, Trinity operates the Illinois Crisis Prevention Network (ICPN), a statewide crisis prevention program, collaboratively with the Hope Institute in Springfield, Illinois.

Well known nationwide for its person-centered culture and employment practices that include such fun activities as Kindness Day and the antics of its mascot Lillie Leapit, Trinity has been recognized with many awards and honors. Among them are the prestigious Alford-Axelson Award for Nonprofit Managerial Excellence, the Psychologically Healthy Workplace Award from the American Psychological Association, and the Silver Stevie Award. Trinity was also included in Richard Steckel's *In Search of America's Best Nonprofits,* and has been recognized by the *Chicago Tribune* as one of Chicago's Top 100 Workplaces.

In addition, the Council on Quality and Leadership has accredited Trinity Services continuously since 1992.

Readers interested in learning more about Trinity Services are invited to visit www.trinityservices.org.

My Plan to
FLOURISH

"The sooner you
start planning your life,
the sooner
you will live the life
you dream of."
—Hans Glint

My Plan to FLOURISH

Doug Blanchard

I AM GRATEFUL

I am grateful for my mom and
dad and my sister Anna.

I am grateful for my job at
Heights Tire Co.

I am grateful for my friends,
especially Jack and Isaac.